guts

guts

The
ENDLESS FOLLIES
and
TINY TRIUMPHS
of a
GIANT DISASTER

KRISTEN JOHNSTON

G

GALLERY BOOKS

New York   London   Toronto   Sydney   New Delhi

G

Gallery Books
A Division of Simon & Schuster, Inc.
1230 Avenue of the Americas
New York, NY 10020

Note to Readers
Some names and identifying details of people portrayed in this book have been changed; in one instance, a character is a composite of two people; and in a few instances, the chronology of events has been slightly altered for pace.

First Gallery Books hardcover edition March 2012

GALLERY BOOKS and colophon are registered trademarks of Simon & Schuster, Inc.

For information about special discounts for bulk purchases, please contact Simon & Schuster Special Sales at 1-866-506-1949 or business@ simonandschuster.com.

The Simon & Schuster Speakers Bureau can bring authors to your live event. For more information or to book an event contact the Simon & Schuster Speakers Bureau at 1-866-248-3049 or visit our website at www.simonspeakers.com.

Designed by Jason Snyder

Manufactured in the United States of America

10 9 8 7 6 5 4 3 2 1

Library of Congress Cataloging-in-Publication Data

Johnston, Kristen
  Guts : the endless follies and tiny triumphs of a giant disaster / by Kristen Johnston.
      p. cm.
  1. Johnston, Kristen, 1967– 2. Actors—United States—Biography.
3. Drug addicts—United States—Biography. I. Title.
    PN2287.J582A3 2012
    792.02'8092—dc23
    [B]
                            2011044413

ISBN 978-1-4516-3505-8
ISBN 978-1-4516-3507-2 (ebook)

THIS BOOK IS DEDICATED TO THE PEOPLE OF LONDON.

ESPECIALLY THE OVERWORKED, UNDERPAID,

TALENTED, AND OCCASIONALLY UNPLEASANT

STAFF OF THE HOSPITAL.

YOU SAVED MY LIFE,

IN WAYS YOU'LL NEVER KNOW.

OH, AND TO ALL THE FREAKS.

YOU KNOW WHO YOU ARE.

The only way to find true happiness is
to risk being completely cut open.

—CHUCK PALAHNIUK

Somebody's boring me—
I think it's me.

—DYLAN THOMAS

contents

introduction

thank you ever so much for buying my book. I feel as if I know you already, and maybe even kind of like you. You certainly have exquisite taste in reading materials. As long as you don't trash me behind my back or send me naked pictures of yourself playing air guitar, we're good. (And, yes, I'm referring to you, inmate 49607.)

I thought it might be best if we got a few things straight before I tell you way more about me than you ever wanted to know. I'd like to start off by vowing to you that every single stupid, funny, tragic, shocking, disgusting, and boring thing in this book really happened to me.

At least, I think so.

No, I'm pretty sure.

You see, there are certain portions of my life that I was wide awake for, yet completely unaware of, even as they were happening. And no, I'm not crazy. Well, that's not really true. I'm not *mental institution* crazy. Yet.

I can't begin to tell you how tempted I am to fill you in on the reason I have such gaping holes in my memory, but I think it's way too early for that. Besides, it's a crucial plot point, and I should probably at least make an effort to build up some dramatic tension before revealing—

Oh, fuck it. I hate waiting. I'm a pill-popping lush.

Your mind is totally blown, isn't it? After all, "an actress addicted to booze and pills" is relatively unheard of. And "an actress addicted to booze and pills who then writes a book about it" is even rarer. And when I say "unheard of" or "rare," what I really mean is "disturbingly com-monplace." It was a dark day indeed when I was forced to admit that I was about as "special" and "unique" as a manila envelope. Even worse, I was beginning to sus-pect that this whole time, my fun, fabulous life was really just one long, meaningless, self-indugent, cliché-ridden thrill ride.

I've been in recovery for five years, and I've worked my ass off to prevent a relapse, but one never knows with something as stupid and annoying as addiction. I could stub my toe, get a papercut, or just be bored and all of a sudden, it's "Has anyone heard from Kristen? She was supposed to be my maid of honor last night and she never showed up."

Because I spent a large extent of my life plowed, you might find yourself longing for more details about certain events. Trust me, so do I. But what am I supposed to do, make shit up? Where's the fun in that?

Certainly, I used to be quite skilled at mild exaggerations to make a story more dramatic or funny. However, I've decided to tell the truth this time, even if it kills me. Mostly because I don't want Oprah to yell at me. (I don't care if she doesn't have a show anymore. She still scares the ever-loving shit out of me.)

Oh, and I've been known to use salty language, but very rarely, and only when it's absolutely fucking necessary.

So that's me. Just your simple, everyday, alcoholic, pill-popping addict-slash-actress who periodically indulges in hyperbole liberally sprinkled with profanities. Translation: I'm a lying drama queen with a dirty yap and a yen for chemicals. Go ahead, say whatever you want about me, because you could never come *close* to what I've said about myself.

I think that about covers it.

You can't say I didn't warn you.

One last quick thing before we begin. I thought this would be a great opportunity to say a simple and heart-felt "thank you" to all of you truly incredible people who are lucky enough to spend your lives in the happy, safe, and lavender-scented meadow of the "nonaddict."

I know I can speak for all of us addicts when I say how deeply grateful we are to all you special souls who aren't addicted to anything. I, for one, feel—

Umm, wait a second—hold on, that doesn't sound quite right. Let me read it again. *Oh, crap.* That's right. I'm *such* a flake. I always seem to forget this one little thing:

guts

You don't *exist*.

Everyone's addicted to something.

Now, before you get your panties in a twist and send me some long, defensive rant (which, by the way, no addict would *ever* do), just hear me out. First of all, I'm willing to admit that there's a very slight possibility I think this way because I live in the Babylon of creativity and mental illness, which is New York City. But, I travel a lot. And I read *In Touch* magazine.

Of course that's not *all* the research I've done on this subject. Don't be ridiculous. I've also spent hundreds of hours exhaustively gathering information from my couch while studiously examining wasted hot messes implode on one of the hundreds of quality "reality" shows offered by almost every single network on television today. That, plus talking to a bunch of people has led me to this completely nonscientific yet chilling conclusion: everyone, absolutely every single postpubescent person in this great nation, *is* or *was* addicted to SOMETHING.

You know, I don't know why people get so touchy about being accused of being an addict in the first place. Like it was some bad thing, when it's really not. In my experience, addicts are usually charming, talented, intelligent, creative, funny, sensitive, and ambitious. I'll admit, this is the case only when they're *not* using. While engaged in their "drug" of choice, addicts are either terrifying, mortifying, or so painfully boring that even their loved ones eventually find themselves praying that they'll have an overdose. (Just a small one. Perhaps a brief coma.)

Oh, please. You know it's true. And who could possibly blame you?

But, dear loved ones, lest you get too excited thinking you've escaped the drug and alcohol curse (so far), do keep in mind that addiction comes in many shapes, sizes, and forms. For example: one fine summer day, you might innocently decide to take a golf lesson. You enjoy it immensely. You then begin to look forward to your Saturday-morning game. Then, without warning, you decide to quit your dental practice, yank your kids from school, load up a moving van, and move everything (including your furious, party-pooper wife) to Arizona.

All so that you can live directly *on* a golf course and satisfy your growing need to play golf every waking minute of every single day.

guts

This, my new friend, is when you no longer play *golf.* Now, it plays *you.*

Ring any bells?

If not, don't worry, I've got another little experiment here that better illustrates my point. Just take a deep breath and ask yourself if you've ever "had an issue" with one or more of the below. The results can be just between the two of us, no one else ever needs to know. And to start things off on the right foot, I'll cop to having issues with eleven of the following, at one time or another:

Drugs, booze, sex, gambling, work, power, religion, shopping, love, cutting or self-harm, food, cleaning, plastic surgery, lip balm (or is this just *me*?), nicotine, television, porn, gossip, winning everything, which is sometimes referred to as being "the best," toxic relationships, sports (playing and/or watching), tattoos, home decor, cars, exercise, money, being right, adrenaline, collecting animals, obsessively collecting anything (dolls, stamps, Hummel figurines, etc.), being too invested in one's kids (with a very special shout-out to all of you stage mothers, you naughty Munchausen syndrome by proxyites, and of course you Little League rage-aholics), makeup, lying, tanning, fame, people addicted to addicts, stimulation, rage, caffeine, and, finally, what I like to refer to as *the umbrella of doom*, under which fall all things computer-related, including the Internet, objects that let you send/receive e-mail, eBay, Facebook, Twitter, online dating, Myspace, Google, and all video games. (Unless it's Tetris, that's perfectly healthy.)

Well, Jesus. I don't know about you, but I'm wiped. I hope I didn't skip anything. I'm not too worried, however. I'm sure if I did, all of you addicts will let me know immediately.

Now here's where it can get quite confusing: many of the above are wonderful and fulfilling activities. A few are necessities. What morphs them into addictions is when they become a habit or an obsession to the extent that they "damage, jeopardize, or shorten one's life. Or when ceasing these behaviors causes physical or psychological trauma."

That definition comes courtesy of Wikipedia, but even that doesn't fully encompass what I understand addiction to be. Scouring the Internet, I couldn't find even *one* definition that fully satisfied me, probably because most of them were more than likely written by well-meaning clinicians who are only addicted to harmless activities such as knitting. (Knitting! How could I have forgotten about those damn knitters?) Therefore, because I'm lucky enough to *be* an addict (which also means I know more about everything than anyone else), I feel compelled to add my own definition. I'm quite proud of it:

> ad·dic·tion [noun]: *When one habitually and obsessively engages in mood-altering behavior that, despite the obliteration of every single thing in their lives they once held dear, they find they simply cannot stop.*—Kristepedia

Pretty good, right? Perhaps you'd like to take a gander at that list again? Seriously, go ahead, I'll wait. I have to call a toxic friend back anyway.

Great. Now, if you can still honestly say to me (well, okay, to my book, but I'll know it if you lie, even if you think I can't see you skulking in the back of that airport bookstore) that you have *never* had an addiction to *any* of the above?

Well, then, I stand corrected. My sincere apologies. You are one lucky soul.

Unfortunately, you also might just be the dullest person alive, and I kind of feel even worse for you than I do for the rest of us lunatics. (And I could *not* agree with you more, hon. This is *so* not the book for you. That new James Patterson hardcover is just two shelves over, you go enjoy.)

Anyone still here?

Oh, goody, let's go.

I got some stories for you.

one

**I SEE NOTHING,
I HEAR NOTHING**

sometimes people's lives change because of the smallest thing: a song, a comment, a fight, a dark night of the soul, or simply a decision.

I'm just a wee bit denser than that. I'm sure that there were many, many signs that I was killing myself, and I was probably given thousands of opportunities to change my life and make it wonderful, but once you've washed down a handful of Vicodin with a bottle or two of a full-bodied cabernet, even reading stop signs while driving a car becomes a tad tricky.

I remember going for week after week to some poor therapist, sobbing about how shitty I felt, how awful my life had become, how alone I was. It did occasionally occur to me that perhaps I should clue her in to the fact that I was a raging alcoholic and drug addict, but I quickly banished that ridiculous thought. That stuff is "private." I learned that a long, long time ago. Instead, I wasted hundreds of her hours (not to mention my cash), asking her (and anyone else stupid enough to be my friend at the time) the one question no one seemed able to answer: "Why, oh why, am I so unhappy?"

On the long, bleak nights when my sorrows and fears were so unbearable that no amount of pills or booze would knock me out, I would stare wide-eyed into the darkness, begging it for an answer. Sometimes a blurry clue would start to form, but just as it started to come into focus, it would disappear, like a ghost. It teased me, always sneakily crawling way back deep inside to snuggle in the dark cavern where I hid all things I deemed "unpleasant," "scary," or "a bummer."

My father used to be obsessed with the TV show *Hogan's Heroes* (alas, now you know the secret inspiration of my subtle comedic choices). There was a stupid, fat German guard named Schultz, who would nervously sing, "I see nothing, I hear nothing!" whenever he was accidentally made privy to the prisoners' weekly escape plans.

guts

Basically, the small remaining part of myself that was still sane became Schultz. Which is not saying all that much for my sanity. I avoided thinking too much about the fact that no matter what I did or how many times I managed to wean myself off pills, eventually I couldn't go more than a few excruciating days without them. Or that I was feeling worse and worse every day, suffering from agonizing bouts of searing heartburn. Or, that I was starting to look really, really bad.

You know, it just occurred to me—I think I was beginning to *look* like Schultz. *Oh my God.* Listen, I wasn't always this way, dammit! I wasn't always some fat Nazi's doppelgänger. I used to be the rowdy, fun girl at the bar, or the dinner party, who was chock-full of sassy, dry witticisms you might chuckle at the next day. I was just very, very *social*, that's all.

Who could've imagined that the totally together, funny, ambitious, generous, and smart girl would slowly morph into a lonely couch potato who spent her free time hiding her wine and pill bottles from her cleaning lady?

I'm pretty sure I've been an addict since I was born, but my love affair with chemicals started in high school. "I can *totally* slam that bottle of Wild Turkey faster than you, entire basketball team!" But, because it ebbed and flowed throughout the years—*hiya, Schultz*—I convinced myself that everything was fine.

Or sort of fine. Kind of. Sometimes.

I mean, when you're in a play and all you care about is where you're getting loaded afterward, that's slightly worrisome. But if you can't fucking *wait* for the fucking audience to get over it and *stop* giving you a standing ovation already, because you're dying to get to the bar? Well, then—that's just a whole other kettle o' crazy.

But it was all I knew, really. Plays were simply a conduit, an appetizer to the most important event of the entire day: *getting hammered.* Endless, sometimes heated arguments between the cast over which place had the best martinis would continue right up until entrances. (And sometimes even beyond.)

Nowadays when I'm in a play, the first thing I do when we move into the theater is to grab a dark red lipstick (frosty pink just doesn't have the same panache) and scrawl in my dressing-room mirror my new mantra:

THIS IS THE MAIN EVENT!

Yeah, yeah, yeah, Shakespeare 'tis not. But that's not the point. You see, *it means something to me.* Besides, "one day at a time," while an excellent motto, doesn't really work for me. I can't help but picture Bonnie Franklin screaming "Schneider!" for the umpteenth time, to canned laughter. You're more than welcome to borrow my mantra, but to be fair I must warn you about a scary potential mind-fuck—which really only applies if you're a gay male and over forty. Whatever you do, please try not to think of the poster for the film *The Main Event*, which showcases a tightly-permed Barbra Streisand in one of the most nauseating costumes in all of celluloid history: boxing shorts and nude pantyhose.

Or, if you *are* gay and over forty, perhaps that would *help*?

Wait. Hold up. Am *I* gay and over forty?

Regardless, I make sure to write THIS IS THE MAIN EVENT! as big as I can, so that as I get ready to go on-stage, I will never again forget how lucky I am to be alive and that I get to do something I love with all my heart.

But back when I was bat-shit crazy, I grew used to waking up having absolutely no recollection of the night before. Every morning, any triumphant performance I may (or may not) have had was consistently diluted by a queasy stomach and a grim fear of the unknown. However, it was far, far worse when I wasn't in a play. Because then I was *bored*. And boredom and addiction are not friends. In fact, they are each other's mortal enemy. It was right around 2001 when every night became lost to me, never to return. Of course, I never *blacked out*. I left that to tacky people and frat boys. I simply drank until I *fell asleep*. And on really naughty nights perhaps I'd oh-so-elegantly *pass out*. And, yes, there's an enormous difference, I'm just still a bit unclear as to what it is.

Soon, I found myself pushing "cocktail hour" earlier and earlier, until three o'clock in the afternoon seemed perfectly reasonable. I wisely took great pains to avoid calling anyone back after 8:00 p.m., realizing that if I couldn't say "Hi, it's Kristen" without it sounding like "HizzKrissen," returning my LA agent's call would perhaps not be a good career move.

Unfortunately, as some of you may already know, one

of the glorious gifts of alcoholism and addiction is a severe lack of discernment. Thankfully, another gift is memory loss, so I'm spared most of my more mortifying drunk-dialing moments. However, I wasn't spared the daily ritual of waking up in the morning only to be slammed with the terrible knowledge that I had called *someone* and, try as I might, I had no recollection of *who* that might have been nor what the *fuck* I had said to them.

I was also becoming hideously bloated, and having long ago been blessed with a face prone to fatness (which my mother would lovingly refer to as "full"), I now had a double chin in all photographs, even while I was looking up. Plus, I started making BIG mistakes. Whoppers. You see, an addict's most important objective in life (after, of course, obtaining their drug of choice) is to convince everyone that they're a happy, healthy person who just enjoys a cocktail or two. That they're "normal." Whatever the hell that means. I still don't know. At any rate, I found myself forgetting important rules that are indispensable to all addicts who'd prefer to avoid an awkward "get-together" with their loved ones and some stranger who's been paid to drag their ass to rehab. Here's a big rule I broke, over and over again: *after the age of twenty-five, women no longer look hot with a red-wine mustache and purple teeth.*

Sorry if you don't like that one, ladies; unfortunately, I have another one just for you: the day you graduate from high school is the day it no longer matters how darling your outfit is or how big your boobs are; *if you slur, girl, you are pathetic.*

You may be thinking, "Well, she's *way* off on that one. I know from firsthand experience that some guys find slurring irresistible." And I wouldn't even think of disagreeing with you, gorgeous. In fact, I'm sure you're right. Only bummer is, they're the kind of guys who prefer to gaze into the whites of women's eyes, think talking's overrated, or trip a woman and laugh hysterically at her when she's on the ground. Which means these heart-stoppers either dislike women, have no teeth, despise women, are on parole, or simply believe women are evil. *For God's sake, scoop him up, girl, what are you waiting for?*

Oh, and don't think I forgot about you gents. While it's frustratingly true that you age far better than we do, if you're over thirty-five and the highlight of your entire year is the day you get to host your office's tailgate party at Lambeau Field, well, that's a bit sad.

However, if you wind up getting so hammered at said party that you poop your pants in front of your ten-year-old son, then welcome to the Land of the Truly Tragic. *Go, Packers.*

This land, also known as Schultz-ville, is a charming enclave where esteem-shattering events become the norm. Picture Mayberry, except that Charlie Sheen is the mayor, Courtney Love is the chief of police, and Lindsay Lohan is the local librarian. Every day is new and exciting.

Want proof? No problem. Just off the top of my head, here are a couple of examples of how awesome this place is: First, *only* in Schultz-ville would it occur to you to give your married boss an impromptu lap dance at your firm's Christmas party (adorable!). It's also the only town I know of where it's just understood that the best place to vomit is right on top of a party's coat bed (bathrooms are a pain in the ass, anyway). Or, for you couch potatoes, another superconvenient vomit receptacle is right in front of your face—the mouth of the girl you're making out with. *(You had me at hello.)*

Still not convinced that this is the greatest place ever?

Good, because I'm not done yet. How would you like to be awoken, instead of by some hideous alarm clock, by screams of rage emanating from the mouth of your ex-girlfriend's father? You greet this fine, sunny day with the dawning revelation that not only have you passed out in the dead center of her family's fancy front lawn but that you've also clearly enjoyed a profound case of explosive diarrhea while doing so. You have no idea how you got there, but it's clear by the faces of the horrified neighbors and her revolted family (not to mention the sound of approaching police sirens) that you'd better skedaddle, but quick!

See what I mean by new and exciting? And it's not even over yet. The cherry on top of this glorious morning is when you get to take the overcrowded forty-five-minute train from Dobbs Ferry to New York City with a broken heart and the most stomach-churning hangover of your life, all while sitting in your own feces.

Man, I love this town. No wonder the population's booming.

By the way, I didn't make any of these up. They're all things that really happened to people I know. If your face is burning with shame or recognition, don't feel too bad.

guts

More than likely, almost everyone you know has spent a nice chunk of time in Schultz-ville.

Or if you were really lucky like me, you had a lovely time-share, right on the beach.

The longer I lived there, however, the worse I felt. And looked. Besides my fat face, double chin, sallow and acne-prone skin, and the fact that my teeth were constantly stained a gorgeous grape color, I soon began to suffer from a lethargy so profound that sometimes the act of brushing my teeth felt like a long day at the office, and I'd fall, winded, back to sleep. Then it started to take me forever just to pee. Eventually it took a twenty-minute ritual of deep breathing combined with the faucet on full force and the latest issue of *O* magazine. Unfortunately, these exhaustive efforts usually resulted in a depressingly sad little trickle.

Plus there was that constant heartburn. Now, the heartburn I'm talking about has nothing to do with those commercials featuring balding, shame-faced men being scolded by their nagging wives for eating too many meatballs. This heartburn meant *business*. The only way I can describe it is . . . imagine a thousand splinters in your throat. Or a hundred paper cuts being doused with lemon juice. Or being forced to listen to Sarah Palin discuss foreign policy. Let's just say it was *exceedingly* uncomfortable. I told myself I must have developed an allergy to some unknown substance (not alcohol, never alcohol), like MSG, tomatoes, or peanuts.

Listen, I wasn't a complete idiot. *Oh, okay, I was.* But I can remember saying to myself quite a few times, "This cannot be good, Kristen. In fact, I think this could be very, very bad."

But most of the time, I was far too busy enjoying the amenities of Schultz-ville. Which, by the way, goes by a lot of different names to a lot of different people. For example, in the Midwest, it's known as Schlitz-ville. Augusten Burroughs calls it *Magical Thinking*, and for Carrie Fisher it's *Wishful Drinking*. My shrink likes to call it denial, but I've told her it just doesn't have the same cozy ring as the others. I don't think it really matters *what* name you call it; the important thing is that we all know how to get there. If only leaving were as easy. Unfortunately, the longer you stay in Schultz-ville, the road out becomes harder and harder to see. Until eventually, it vanishes.

But what did I care? While there, I didn't waste my

time thinking about icky things like *going to rehab* or *dying*. I would simply crack open my second bottle of merlot and revel in the lonely luxury of being able to concentrate on truly meaningful and challenging things, such as mastering the increasingly difficult and decreasingly rewarding art of "feeling better."

I became a master of this delicate and oft-misunderstood life skill. I'll admit, it's not as lofty as curing cancer, but the dedication it takes to procure drugs, understand dosages, obsessively count pills so you know exactly when you'll run out, and keep track of *which* doctors know *what* story, *what* pharmacy has filled *which* prescription *when*—well, I think it's fair to say healthy amounts of organizational prowess, intelligence, and people skills are needed to be as successful at drug addiction as I was. I was also a pretty damn good liar, which didn't hurt. Somehow, I managed to keep my addiction a secret from everyone (other than those who really knew me, but most of the time, even they only had niggling suspicions or a vague feeling that something was off).

My real triumph (if you could call it that) was that somehow, the press never found out. No *TMZ* footage of me leaving Bungalow 8 with white powder on my upper lip. And that's not just luck, my friends, that takes some serious skill. (It was mostly luck.)

I may have been adept at the art of addiction, but unfortunately, this also meant that for many years I was a card-carrying member of what is referred to as "functioning addicts," which, trust me, is the very worst kind. You see, we "functioning addicts" devote so much time and energy toward keeping our addictions alive, happy, and well fed, by the time we've made that oh-so-subtle shift to "nonfunctioning addict," our brains are so fried we're incapable of grasping the concept that things have shifted drastically, and not in our favor. We have absolutely no ability to see the desolate disaster our lives have become, how many family, friends, and lovers we've lost, or how close to death we actually are. Judgment has disappeared along with everything else good in our lives, and *we simply cannot stop.*

It felt like I was speeding on the Autobahn toward hell, trapped inside a DeLorean with no brakes. And even if I *could* somehow stop, I'd still be screwed, because there's no way I'd ever be able to figure out how to open those insane, cocaine-designed doors.

guts

It was indescribably awful. I felt no hope, no joy, no nothing.

Only a powerful and all-consuming hatred for my own guts.

Which is especially fascinating when you take into consideration that my guts hated me right back, a fact I became aware of only when they blew themselves up in a brutal and shocking act of revenge.

Well played, guts. Well played.

two

THE FREAK
HAS LANDED

In 1967, my beautiful parents had been blessed with a gorgeous and brilliant blond boy, so they rolled the dice, knowing that a darling, well-behaved little girl would be the perfect addition to their charming, sunny family. Too bad that what they got was a loud, cantankerous, funny, moody, weepy, dramatic, temperamental, ornery, and occasionally truly awful little girl with a fondness for both drooling and screaming *"No!"* at every opportunity. Eventually my parents did get their sweetheart of a daughter, my beautiful younger sister, Julie.

But it was too late. The Freak had landed. In her very own DeLorean.

_____

". . . And then you'll all walk, single file, into the church for the graduation ceremony!" Sister Anita breathlessly finished, her face aglow with excitement.

Right on cue, Sarah Smith shot her annoying hand into the air. "How will we know the order of the procession?" (She was not only charmless, but wore a scoliosis back brace *and* had a lisp. So she pronounced it "protheth-on." We ate lunch together every day. Not by choice.)

I'm sure Sister Anita found Tharah Thmith to be as irritating as the rest of us, but because she was having a passionate love affair with Jesus, she instead replied, "Well, isn't that a *wonderful* question, Sarah! You'll be entering the church according to height. Shortest first, meaning the girls, of course! And then finishing with the tallest, you boys."

Uh-oh. That finally got my attention. I looked up from my notebook, where I had been drawing a bunch of different eyeballs. All the air had left the room, and everyone, even Sister Anita, was suddenly wondering the same thing: *Where the holy hell do we put the Freak?*

It was a beautiful and unseasonably warm April day

guts

in 1980, and we were discussing the details of our grade-school graduation. I had just slogged through a painful, confusing, and mostly pretty unhappy eight years at a Catholic grade school, located in a gorgeous and wealthy suburb of Milwaukee, Wisconsin. In a few months, to my everlasting relief and excitement, I'd be attending a *public* high school, which meant no more endless hours spent in the hideous beige-brick church (conveniently attached to the hideous beige-brick school), no more nuns who thought I not only had "terrible social skills" and an "unpleasant disposition" but that I also was "very difficult to teach." (They left out terrible bowler, serial arsonist, mouth-breather, and kitten killer.)

My parents had the very best of intentions when they sent all three of their kids to this particular school, which was renowned for its academic excellence. What they couldn't have known was that it was also hell on earth if you weren't friends with the "in" people, didn't wear the "in" clothes, didn't have the "in" haircut, and weren't blessed with a perfect chin that would jut out charmingly whenever one would utter such bons mots as "Eau my Gaud, Stacy. Can you *even believe* she wore that sweater *again*? It is *the* ugliest thing I have *ever* seen."

Looking back, I do find it a bit fascinating that such a large percentage of this supposedly religious school's student body was made up of kids whose behavior I'm pretty sure would've bummed Jesus right out. So after eight long years, I graduated with a boatload of self-esteem issues and a profound mistrust of Catholicism. Not quite what my parents had hoped for, I'm sure.

Of course, not *all* of the kids were awful. Many were downright lovely, in fact. And I do have some nice memories of my time spent at this school. For instance, one year I WON the science-fair contest with my best friend, Heather (one of the lovely ones). She and I spent an entire afternoon figuring out how to make paper from scratch. I'm still a bit lost as to why we won, but it was the only time in all of grade school that I felt kind of smart. (Even if I did nothing but dramatically read aloud the directions from some book as I ate Fig Newtons.)

If you'd like a crack at winning *your* science fair, here's the recipe! Simply ask Heather's mom to mash wood chips in a blender until it almost breaks, add some other gunk, have her bake it for a long time, and then lay the whole mess out to dry for two days on the deck. The end result should closely resemble a stucco ceiling. You're quite welcome!

My brother was a few grades above me, a brilliant, shy, sensitive virtuoso violinist, and I absolutely, unabashedly worshipped him. Regrettably, this was not a feeling shared by his classmates, and he was tortured so viciously, so relentlessly, it must have really done a number on him. But that's just a guess. We've never spoken about it. All I know is bearing witness to it sure did a number on *me*.

For years, I saw him verbally attacked, punched, slapped, tripped, shoved, and once even hung up on a tree by the band of his underwear. My heart absolutely shattered for him, over and over, but I was never able to tell him this without sounding like an irritating younger sister. Eventually, I learned not to discuss it with him, or anyone else.

Everything changed one dark and miserable autumn day when I was around nine. I was daydreaming my way through some boring class when suddenly we were all jolted by a scream of pure terror coming from outside. My blood immediately ran cold. *Was that my brother?* We all ran to the huge window overlooking the football field and, despite the teacher's protestations, pressed our faces against the glass.

At first, my mind couldn't understand what it was seeing. But within seconds I realized that it was a mob of four or five boys attacking someone. The frenzy had whipped up a large mass of dust and dirt, and I remember the child part of my brain thinking, *"Pig-Pen,"* at the very same moment my brand-new, maturing part thought, *They're killing my brother.* I'd never seen him being assaulted like this. I honestly thought he was being murdered, right before my eyes. I was incapacitated, unable to move or speak.

"Oh, my dear God!" the teacher cried as she ran for help, which broke the spell. One of my classmates giggled nervously, and it was at that moment my grief and fear thankfully crystallized into a swirling ball of volcanic fury.

The "Pig-Pen" incident was the catalyst for a completely impetuous and ill-advised decision, the first of many I would continue to make throughout my life. It happened

guts

a month or two later, just after the first light snowfall, and it was the end of recess. The bell had rung and most of the kids had already dutifully filed back indoors. I was dawdling along as usual, lost in thought. Then, just as I reluctantly started to yank the door open, I saw a flash of a reflection in the glass of someone far behind me. There was no mistaking who it was. Danny "Sully" Sullivan, hockey player, choirboy, and my brother's most dedicated tormentor. He was a massive, stupid, doughy kid with bright red hair, freckles, and pooh-colored eyes that almost masked his budding psychosis. Despite the brisk temperature, he was wearing shorts, plodding gracelessly across the cement toward the doors with a football in his giant hand. That's when it occurred to me that we were alone.

The molten ball of rage that had been lying dormant for weeks instantly came alive, and all I knew was that somehow, some way, I had to find a way to release it. That's when I found myself exceedingly grateful for the very thing I'd always been most ashamed of (until then, that is). I had fucked-up feet. I almost smiled. Because from the time I was six or seven, I had been forced to wear hideous corrective shoes due to my excessively high arches. Without them, my feet tended to roll inward, which would then cause my knees to bash into each other. All in all, not a flattering look. Therefore, instead of the soft Docksiders everyone else wore, I was doomed to wear these very strong, resilient, and quite unbecoming shoes called brogues (which ironically originated in Sully's ancestral homeland of Ireland). Oh, how I loathed those shoes. Until that day, that is.

Even though adrenaline was coursing through my body, I patiently waited until he was right next to me. He barely glanced at me, the awkward, spindly girl with the spaghetti legs poking out of her huge plaid uniform. Then, when he was close enough for me to smell his sour sweat, the volcano blew. With all the rage in my black heart, almost as if I was possessed by the Bionic Woman or the Incredible Hulk, I kicked his shin as hard as I could with the reinforced toe of my sturdy shoe.

I can still hear the loud *thewwack!* that reverberated across the pavement when my foot connected with his bare shin. It sounded as if I had hit a coconut with a two-by-four. I kicked him so hard my right leg trembled for days afterward. He immediately dropped the football and bent over, screaming in agony, and grabbed his fat, already-bruising shin.

Then he looked up at me and screamed, *"Wh-h-y-y???!"*

He was crying. I had made Danny Sullivan, the scariest kid in school, the boy even the male teachers couldn't make eye contact with, weep like a girl. For a split second I just stood there, in absolute shock. Of course, I instantly burst ino tears and ran inside and down the hall as fast as my Irish corrective shoes would carry me.

"You won't like me when I'm angry. . . ."

Unfortunately, when word got to my brother, he was so mortified that he stopped speaking to me for a long, long time. (Who could blame him? I mean, your little sister trying to slay your dragon? NOT COOL.) I wished I could find the words to explain to him that I couldn't help it, that it was for me as much as for him, but, as usual, they never came.

It was a few months later, on an ice-cold but gorgeous Saturday in February, and long after I had dropped my guard, when Sully exacted his revenge. I was skating with a bunch of kids on the enormous neighborhood pond.

Heather, Tharah, and myself were playing "Olympics," which meant we were engaged in a very tight battle for the ladies' short-program gold medal. Due to her lisp and her ever-present back brace, Tharah made a brilliant (and hilarious) Russian judge. I was about to execute a very tricky triple axel (which meant hopping to one skate and holding up your other leg until it burned), when an odd hush descended over the entire pond.

I looked around at the crowd of kids, puzzled. A feeling of foreboding crackled through the cold air. Just then, I thought I caught a glimpse of bright red hair. I barely had time to think, *Hey, that's weird. Doesn't he usually skate in the hockey rink?* when my mouth went dry. Not only was it *him*, but he was with four other huge boys, and they were all casually holding their hockey sticks as they slowly skated toward me.

I was stock-still, unable to move as everyone else vanished like smoke. *They couldn't be here to hurt me, there are parents here,* I thought desperately. As they came closer, and I saw their cold black eyes, I was finally galvanized to move and my trembling legs began to skate away from them as fast as they could. Unfortunately, this meant that I was skating farther and farther away from the tiny lodge where the parents could see us. I was so eager to get away from them, I didn't realize this fatal mistake until it was too late.

Within minutes I was at the far edge of the pond and I was caught. Towering over me were fir trees and five enormous bullies. There was nowhere else to go. I just stood there, shivering from the cold and terror as Sully skated up to me. I closed my eyes as Sully, without even saying a word, made a fist and punched me with all the brute force he possibly could.

Except he didn't punch my face as I was grimly expecting. Instead, his massive fist plowed, with the force of a battering ram, directly into my nine-year-old vagina. The impact swooped me up into the air and flipped me over into the snowbank, barely missing a tree. I gracelessly landed in a heap, the wind knocked out of me. When I could finally breathe, I curled into a tight ball of pain and shame, my mittened hands holding my throbbing crotch. Eventually, tears streaming down my face, I looked up to see the five boys laughing, the setting sun making them glow like angels.

In my school, you were considered "out" if you wore the wrong brand of socks. Therefore, due to my penchant for footwear that made me look like a Scottish golfer and because I was a book-loving, "learning disabled" theater geek with a loud mouth, I think it's safe to say I didn't come close to being "in."

However, I soon discovered being "out" was the least of my problems. When I was around ten years old, something unsettling began to occur that transported me way, way beyond the world of "out" and crash-landed me directly onto planet "Freak." Up until then, I was average height, same as everyone else. But overnight I started to grow. And grow. And just when I thought it was over, I'd relax, thinking, *Thank God THAT's over with!* I'd suddenly begin to grow some more. I grew so furiously, so relentlessly that by the time I was twelve, I was almost six feet tall, the height I am now. I towered over every single person at the school, even the priests. My ever-lengthening shins and forearms would actually hurt from growing, and the bigger I got, the more I'd slouch, praying I would appear smaller. Unfortunately, all this did was make me look like a giant Freak with crappy posture.

It was so worrisome that I recall being driven by my

sobbing mother (in her fur coat over her tennis whites) from Milwaukee to Chicago so I could see a specialist because she and my father were worried that I was literally becoming a *giant*. As in one of those eight-foot-tall people who have funny voices and have to have clothes especially made for them.

To my mother's eternal relief, I wasn't a giant. To my soul-crushing horror, I was simply a Freak. At least, that's what I secretly called myself. I was the master tormentor of my own mind, a bully toward myself so hateful and venomous I even rivaled Amy Grable, who had somehow become the undisputed ruler of the vast kingdom known as grade school. To this day, I don't think I've ever met anyone so powerful, manipulative, and compelling in my entire life. And I'm in *show biz*, for Christ's sake. I'm not sure which came first: Amy's derision toward me or my hatred for myself. I suppose it doesn't really matter. My self-esteem was utterly decimated by both of us.

There is nothing like the absolute power we give to the cruel when we're young. Somehow, as if our whole grade were filled with tiny Squeaky Frommes, we all just accepted that Amy was our QUEEN, simply because she said it was so. We were her mere disciples, there to do her bidding and (for a tiny faction that included Tharah and myself) to be available at all times for her torture. Like all good/evil queens, the gods had smiled upon her in almost every way. She had perfect teeth; full, glossy lips; long, shimmering blond hair (that I'm still convinced she got professionally blown out every morning); alabaster skin; long legs; and, at an outrageously young age, proudly displayed a set of real, honest-to-goodness boobs (not the Kleenex-in-the-bra boobs like the rest of us). It didn't matter what sex you were, you could simply not refrain from openly soaking in her Amy-ness. She only had two minor drawbacks. She was dumb as a box of hammers and mean as a snake.

It was Amy who first anointed me "the Jolly Green Giant," which is not all that much better than "the Freak," if you ask me. I'll never forget her constant greeting to me: "Hey, Jolly Green Giant, how's the weather up there?" or, on uniform-free social occasions, "Looks like the Jolly Green Giant's expecting a flood!" and on and on. These comments were always followed by gales of laughter from her subjects. Seems stupid, and even rather banal, I know. But I couldn't help how tall I was, so to have it shoved in my face over and over, every single day, for years, created a sense of self-disgust that would haunt me for years.

Because my existence was beginning to resemble a never-ending game of Pin the Tail on the Freak, one could hardly blame me for escaping whenever possible. I did this by existing almost 100 percent of the time in my imagination. I spent almost every single class from grade school through high school lost in a safe world of my making. Even then, I couldn't bear to be present or fully in my own skin. Even then, I couldn't wait to be *other*.

Only recently has it dawned on me that this was unusual behavior.

I'd pay attention in English and history classes, or if I liked a teacher. But most of the time, the bell would ring, I'd look down at my book, and I'd be gone, totally gone, for the next hour. Sometimes my fantasies would be sort of conventional, like I'd be a rock star's girlfriend. (I've always had a preference for the drummers, don't know why.) Sometimes I'd enter the world of whatever book I was reading at the time. Sometimes I'd be an actress in

New York *dating* a drummer. But my most common fantasy was much simpler: I'd be the new girl at my school, my name would be something normal like Becky or Lisa, and I'd be so teeny-tiny and gosh-darned cute that people couldn't resist picking me up and kissing my adorable cheeks when they passed me in the hallway. Even Amy would invite me over for a swim in her new pool.

Unfortunately, I was *other* so often that eventually I was sent to special classes for kids with learning disabilities. Which gave me another endearing moniker: "Retard." I remember crying into my pillow many nights, railing at God, *Now I'm retarded* and *a giant? What's next, Lord, epilepsy?* The good Lord surprised me by bellowing, *Certainly, why not, ye Freak?*

And thus, from age seven to twelve or so, I had epileptic seizures. I don't remember much about them, only that one second everything would be normal, and the next second I'd be on the ground, kids would be crying and staring at me, and a horrified Father Ryan would have his meaty paw wrapped around my tongue to prevent me from choking. One time, I remember riding my bike home from school when it happened. I came to just as a terrified woman was rushing to me from her car, thinking she had hit me. I played it off, saying I must have hit an unseen bump and I was fine. I walked the rest of the way home on rubbery legs and never told a soul. Strangely, the seizures stopped forever right around the time I left grade school.

Despite that my life at this point was sort of a bummer (for an upper-middle-class, Midwestern kid with plenty to eat, lots of fun vacations, a beautiful home, and parents who loved her, that is), I knew something none of my classmates did. Deep inside, I knew someday I'd win. Because only I knew that the girl they loved to make fun of, the girl who was only invited to slumber parties when they were absolutely forced to, the girl who always said the wrong thing at the worst possible moment— only I knew that this girl, this stupid, spindly stick figure with a terrible personality actually disguised a future FAMOUS ACTRESS. Or FAMOUS PHOTOGRAPHER. Sometimes it was FAMOUS MODEL. And sometimes, it was simply a *FAMOUS PERSON*. If I was *FAMOUS*, it would mean that I was *NOT ME*, which would, in turn, make me *HAPPY*.

Finally, when I began my last year of grade school, things began to get somewhat better. Just as Dorothy discovered at the end of *Oz*, it was all because of a gift that I'd had all along and never fully appreciated. It was a weapon I soon discovered was even more powerful than being petite, pretty, smart, or popular. *I was funny.*

I had spent years entertaining my family and a few friends with wisecracks, or convincing my poor sister to perform in comedic masterpieces (written, directed, and of course, starring me) for our mom and dad and our neighbor Bitsy, but I had no clue that being funny was a skill that *other* people would like.

I don't remember the exact event, but when I eventually discovered by accident that if I was funny at school, not only would people like me more but I would be protected from most of the torment (at least, where it mattered the most, on the outside). This is where I began my love affair with self-deprecation, which quite clearly continues to this very day.

I found it mind-blowing that if I made fun of myself *first* (and better), it would remove all the power from those about to make fun of *me*. This was a total revelation. After *years* of begging my confused mother to buy me the "sweater with the tiny polo player, not the sweater with the tiny alligator!," after thousands of hours spent trying to look a certain way or be a certain way, or talk a certain way—I just couldn't fucking believe it. This whole time it had been *this easy*?

Finally, one day in eighth grade, just before graduation, I had had enough of the Dictatorship of Amy. I was in the crowded cafeteria, probably eating something gross and trying to crack people up, when I felt Her Highness approach, surrounded by her ever-present cult of slightly less attractive but just as evil girls.

As she began to say, "How's the—"

I knew I couldn't bear to hear it even one more time. I stood up quickly, which caused her to step back in fear. Emboldened, I loudly said, "Amy, on behalf of the entire school, I really think you should at least *try* to think of something else to say, because I would hate for people to wonder if maybe you're dumb."

What I really said might have been somewhat lamer, but in my memory, that's what I said. After a weighty moment of stunned silence, I heard a twitter. Then a snort. Then full-out laughter, which has always been my very favorite sound in the whole wide world. It filled me with such joy because, for once, it wasn't directed *at* me, it was *because* of me. Even Amy's cohorts snickered until she glared at them. I wish I could say I was never teased again. I was still made fun of, but much, much less often. Amy pretended I didn't exist.

Finally, graduation came. A perfect procession of tiny girls all in white dresses, followed by slightly taller boys in their smart blue blazers and ties. And right there, dead center, was a giant Freak. But for once I didn't care. People could stare all they wanted, because never again would I have to sit through a plodding, endless mass right before lunchtime as my stomach made embarrassingly loud noises (the cafeteria was helpfully located directly *beneath* the church). Never again would I have to be taught English by a nun who knew less about books than I did. Never again would I want to die of shame as the loudspeaker screamed, *"Miss Johnston, please report to your special education class,"* to the entire school. And never, ever again would I have to see Amy Grable. Apparently, she was sent to an all-girls Catholic high school, where I'm sure she continued mastering the fine art of torturing the special and unique.

guts

About thirteen years ago, on a break from filming *3rd Rock from the Sun* in LA, I came back to Milwaukee for Christmas break. It was snowing like crazy, and out of boredom Julie and I decided to go to the local mall. Suddenly, I heard a scream so high-pitched and loud that I almost dropped my Orange Julius.

"Oh. My. Gaaaad!"

I quickly turned around and saw a very overweight woman with pockmarked skin and dirty-blond hair pointing at me, her mouth open. Even from fifteen feet away I could see she lived by the bold but erroneous credo "The more makeup you have on your face, the less people will look at your ass."

From the extreme volume of her voice and the feverishly excited look in her eyes, I assumed she must be a *huge* fan of *3rd Rock*, and I promptly put my "gracious and charming" face on. That's when Julie, who has an encyclopedic recollection of almost everyone who's ever lived in the greater Milwaukee area, urgently whispered, "Wait, Kristen!"

"What?" I said, smile planted on, as the woman hustled toward us.

"That's Amy O'Connor, she used to be Amy Grable."

"Wha . . . ?"

Holy crap. I stopped in my tracks. "Used to be" was a mammoth understatement. This hideously over-made-up horror show bore zero resemblance to the gorgeous girl I had always secretly held up as the Ideal of Beauty.

Amy hugged me. Hard. For a long time. A *very, very* long time. I looked at my sister for help, but she was hysterically laughing behind a fake bush. My eyes watered as the overwhelming combination of body odor and Elizabeth Taylor's White Diamonds singed my nostril hairs. Thankfully, she finally released me, and then giddily introduced me to her two sullen boys.

There was an awkward pause. I glared at the bush. *Julie, you are fucking dead in two minutes.* That's when Amy did something I shall never, ever forget as long as I live. She fished around in her enormous purse and took out a pen and a receipt. *Oh, no, please not my number,* I thought as she held them out to me. But then, as if she were terrified of being rude (oh, trust me, doll, that ship has sailed), she asked me for my autograph.

I was silent for a moment.

"Of course, why not?" I replied magnanimously, while inside I was screaming, *Haha, hahaha, you ugly cow! I win! I win! Ding, dong, the queen is dead!* I wrote:

> Dear Amy—
> It must really suck to know
> you peaked at twelve.
> love, Kristen

Oh, come on—I'm kidding! I would never do that, mostly due to the woman standing right in front of me. Because of her, I have an intimate understanding of how utterly devastating words can be. Besides, my mama raised me better than that. Instead, I wrote:

> Amy—
> Great to See you!
> love, Kristen

She lumbered happily away. Sensing I was going into shock, Julie sat me down on a cement bench outside the Gap. *I just can't believe it.*

"I'm getting a fake tattoo, want one?" Julie asked.

I shook my head. "I just can't believe it."

"What, how fat she is?"

"No. Well, yes. But mostly I can't believe that for the very first time since *grade school*, I'm so grateful I'm not her."

Julie laughed. "Well, *duh!*" and walked over to the tattoo stand.

But Julie had been pretty, petite, kind, and popular. Therefore, one would think I would have despised her or at the very least been eaten alive with jealousy. However, even though Julie may have looked like an angel, she'd also been blessed with the dirtiest mouth of anyone I've ever met in my life. And the fact that she thought I was the funniest human alive didn't hurt, either. Regardless, despite how cool Julie was, there was no possible way I could explain how I felt to a girl who had once been crowned homecoming queen.

As I sat there on that cement bench, next to a plastic fern, it struck me that maybe I *had* triumphed, after all. Not because of dumb stuff like looks or fame or success. Or even lack of body odor. Maybe I had triumphed because instead of crushing me, this person had unwittingly forced me to become someone *interesting*. A person who knows that the greatest curse in life is when it's handed to you on a silver platter. Someone who knows it's so much better to have to *fight* for what you want. Someone who understands that the more people tell you you're going to fail, the more you're driven to prove them wrong. And at the end of the day, *funny and interesting* will always kick *pretty and perfect*'s ass.

I mean, think about it—if there weren't people like *her* to torture people like *me*, would people like me even *exist*?

Now, I wish what I'd written was this:

Dearest Amy,
Thank you, from the
bottom of my heart.
Love,
The Freak

three

Kristen Johnston 1984-1985

NAME

WHITEFISH BAY
HIGH SCHOOL

TOWER TIMES	ATHLETICS
YEARBOOK	RECREATION

10 11 12

ANYONE BUT ME

I think once you've been different, you remain overly sensitive to being labeled for the rest of your life. After all, isn't *label* just a fancy word for *name-calling*? I've always found it kind of weird that even though I was incessantly bullied about it throughout childhood and am still reminded of it constantly to this day, my height never occurs to me until someone says something. Which is daily. I'll be innocently walking my dog, Pinky, and some dashing gent will walk by me and feel the need to say, "Damn, you one *BIG* girl!" and only then will I think, *Oh, that's right. I'm not normal. I'm one BIG girl.* The only other time it occurs to me is when I'm talking to another tall person, but even then it's only because I'm thinking, *Well,* *isn't that nice, my neck doesn't hurt!* And then, as she walks away, I think smugly, *Damn, she is one BIG girl.*

We like to assume we outgrow labels when we become grown-ups. But for most of us, it's just not true. "The Goth" has become "The Soccer Mom." "The Nerd" has blossomed into "The Rich Guy Married to a Playboy Bunny." "The Bad Boy" is now "A Registered Sex Offender." And "The Football Hero" has sadly become "A Fat Drunk." I do it, too. It's human nature, I guess. It's easier for us to put a label on someone; for some weird reason it makes us feel better about ourselves. As if putting others in a definable little box gives us power over them and keeps us from having to look at ourselves. It prevents us from admitting that we're miserable in our own skin. Just like in high school, labels are always said with a hint of derision and judgment. "She's just an *artist*"; "He's *really gay*"; "There goes that *hick*"; or "Damn, that is one *BIG* girl."

I can't remember my first drink. All I know about alcohol was that, like the perfect pair of Levi's, it felt as if it had been there my whole life. I loved drinking, being drunk, and all drunk people. Suddenly, my voice *wasn't* the loudest in the room, and my terrible habit of blurting out comments without editing them first was now "the funniest thing ever!"

Once I got to high school in the early eighties, I worked very hard to make sure I was no longer the Jolly Green *anything*. I was now the Party Animal/Drama Nerd! I know, I know, they don't usually go together. But I think I made it work beautifully. For example, when I played Smitty in *How to Succeed in Business Without Really Trying*, I always had a loud, drunken cheering section. Since then, I've always had a soft spot in my heart for a tipsy audience.

Things had definitely improved since grade school, but physically I was still a disaster. I was never the girl boys liked. I became the girl boys talked to *about* the girl they liked. I can't imagine why. After all, what's hotter than an enormous, sexless loudmouth with a bad perm who can outdrink the entire football team? Blind fools.

In my high school, drinking was just what everyone did. Because I grew up just outside of the city known as "the beer capital of the universe," all one needed to buy a six-pack of beer was two dollars and a hilariously bad fake ID. In the eighties, all this entailed was writing *1965* with a black marker over *1967* on your driver's license. There weren't a lot of drugs around, just a little pot, but there was always booze, and lots of it. We mostly drank on the weekends, but as I got older, it became more pervasive. By the time I was a senior, birthdays were just an excuse for all of us to get breakfast at the local Howard Johnson. We would all pour vodka into our glasses of orange juice under the table, and then go to school hammered. I'm not quite sure what the point was; however, we thought it was just fantastic.

I still loved acting, even more than drinking. Most of the time. Even though my biggest dream of becoming a FAMOUS ACTRESS was still all-consuming, over the years I had tacked on another goal: to someday move to my favorite city in the universe, New York, and then become a FAMOUS ACTRESS. When I was a kid, I loved Judy Blume books, but not for the mild pornographic elements that intrigued everyone else. I would read them because they were either set in New York, or in New Jersey, which was right next to New York. In high school, countless hours of *other* were devoted to imagining my future life there.

Even with my continued devotion to *other*, I somehow managed to just scrape through math and science, and for a "former retard" I scored high enough on the SATs to get into NYU's Tisch School of Drama. Two of my dreams were coming true: I was going to learn how to become a FAMOUS ACTRESS, and I was living in my dream city while doing it.

It was on my very first day of NYU that my life and goals changed forever. That was the day I met the most magical, complicated, and influential man of my life: David. He was my age, but far smarter and turned me on to all things brilliant and fabulous and funny. He was terrifyingly smart, and no one I have ever met in my life has ever made me laugh harder than he did. He adored the film critic Pauline Kael and introduced me to Hitchcock, Douglas Sirk, Robert Altman, John Cassavetes, and Brian De Palma. I'm only slightly ashamed to say that my happiest memories of college were spent in his dorm room (usually smoking pot), watching movies like *Mommie Dearest, Imitation of Life, The Fan, Dressed to Kill, The*

Exorcist, and *Eyes of Laura Mars*. He remains to this day my favorite stage actor of all time. I sometimes wonder what kind of boring actress I'd be if I hadn't met him.

Apropos of nothing, he was the first man to ever tell me I was beautiful. He was gay, but when you've spent your whole life desperately wishing someone would saw your legs off at the knee, a compliment's a compliment. Up until then, I had been saddled with the one label all girls fear: I had a "good personality." Ick. Translation: I was funny, smart, and repulsive. Once I moved to New York City, however, my height started to become a positive thing. It took a while for it to sink in. A tiny, adorable girl would come up to me at a party and say, "I would give *anything* to be your height!" and it was only after I'd say, "Shut the fuck up, you midget bitch," and she'd burst into tears, that I understood that she'd *meant it*.

It was also in New York that I discovered that having a good personality was, in itself, an attractive quality. I was starting to blossom, *finally*. By the time I was in my early twenties, and if I was having an especially good hair day, I could (if one squinted) be described as "decent looking" and occasionally even "striking." Okay, only my mom called me striking. But gay men? Gay men used words like "gorgeous!," "stunning!," and "beautiful!" Which might have something to do with why my relationships with gay men tend to be more successful than my relationships with straight men.

And it all started with David. Also because of him, my ambition slowly morphed into a fierce desire to *be good*. Which, I suppose, included famousness, but to me all that really meant at the time was that people would compliment me a lot, and that I could afford a summer home in Maine.

Looking back, I think one of the happiest times in my life was after NYU, when I was a "Waitress-Slash-Out-of-Work Actor." Everyone I knew was in the same boat, so it was a tight club of warriors whose members included just about everyone I loved. And hated. And was jealous of. And was proud of. And hated.

We all worked our asses off. We'd hold down miserable jobs and spend every free moment hanging our own lights in some Lower East Side, rat-infested shithole, handing out flyers, headshots, and meager résumés to anyone we could. I was a member of the Atlantic Theater

Company, which is now a massively successful and powerful theater and production company. But back then, things were very different. We'd spend our summers in Vermont, producing and acting in plays, and sometimes bringing a play back to New York.

There were three gorgeous blondes in Atlantic who had seniority over me, which meant for four or five years I was Cinderella. I'd be the prop girl, or the assistant director, or sometimes run lines with one of the blondes. Sometimes I was thrown a bone and at the end of the summer I'd be given a role or two in the annual evening of one acts, which is where the playwright Howard Korder saw me perform.

Thank God he did, because when I was twenty-four, he gave me my first "big break." He decided to let Atlantic produce his brilliant new play *The Lights*, and only because of his insistence that I get cast in one of the pivotal roles. "Rose" was an exceptional part—a bossy, mean, sad, funny, very angry lush. Surprisingly, the role fit me like a glove. We did it in Burlington, Vermont, and I was just ecstatic. I remember thinking, *There's nothing that can top this!*

Turns out, as usual, I was wrong. The producers from

the Lincoln Center Theater, Bernie Gersten and André Bishop, came up to Vermont to see *The Lights* and decided to move it right into their small theater, the Mitzi Newhouse, at LINCOLN EFFING CENTER! It wasn't a smashing success, but it was the moment I was sure I was finally *making it*. I was right this time.

Someone from the Carsey-Werner Company (producers of shows like *Roseanne* and *That '70s Show*, among many others) came to New York and decided to see the play. The next day, he called my agent to say they were developing a show in the next year or two that starred John Lithgow as an alien and that I might be right for one of the roles. *Wait a minute, sir. Are you saying that in a year, I'd MAYBE be allowed to audition to play an alien with that creepy guy from* Cliffhanger *and* Raising Cain? *What an honor, I'll just sit here and wait for your call!*

Yeah, right, like that would ever happen.

And of course, because I'm always wrong, it did. Once *3rd Rock* became a huge success, one would think that I would've been giddy to be showered with the labels that came next. Especially after working so hard. I mean, *hello*! Who the hell wouldn't? Therefore, imagine my overwhelming confusion and crushing disappointment when I discovered that the words "famous," "star," or "celebrity" did not suit me at all. In fact, all they really left me with was an overpowering fear that people would discover what I *really* was: a Freak in sheep's clothing. They're labels that bring to mind the kind of gorgeous, perfect, soulless, egomaniacal, self-absorbed people I laugh at and judge just as harshly as you.

Not only that, but it always felt as if they must be talking about some stranger, a fur-sheathed glamour-puss who gets a French mani/pedi every morning, has an entire closet devoted simply to her shoes, and pettily tosses her hairbrush at her maid's skull whenever the mood strikes her. I found myself wishing I could go back, that this wasn't the answer at all.

One of the most unsettling aspects was to suddenly be considered a babe. After a lifetime of knowing I was a dog, when scripts for *3rd Rock* would say, "All the men can't speak, Sally's so hot" or "Sally enters. Jaws drop" and the like, I was honestly baffled and terrified. I was positive that one day the producers would wake up and think, *What the fuck are we* doing? *Let's see if Brooke Shields or someone* actually *hot is available!* And I'd immediately be shipped back to dogtown, where I belonged.

guts

Don't get me wrong, I loved doing *3rd Rock*. The acting part. It was just everything else that came with it that threw me for a big fat loop. Honestly, I suppose I just didn't think the whole "famous" thing through well enough. I assumed that one could be "famous" whenever one felt like it, then go back to normal the rest of the time. It was a sad day when I had to acknowledge that I loved everything about being a FAMOUS ACTRESS except the FAMOUS part.

I'm quite aware that it's probably a bit of a stretch for anyone to feel any sympathy for the trials and tribulations of being "famous," in fact, I think I just vomited a little in my mouth, so I won't loiter here long. But before I move on, have any of you ever marveled at the sheer number of "famous" people who, since pretty much the dawn of show biz, have been cursed with drug addiction, sex addiction, or alcoholism? Or who've purposely sabotaged a career most people would (and do) murder to have? Or who've died a horrible, early death? Very often all of the above?

It has definitely struck *me*, but then one of my favorite books of all time is *Hollywood Babylon* by Kenneth Anger. When a highly sensitive person with low self-esteem and a deep-seated need for approval becomes overnight famous, is suddenly "celebrated" everywhere they go, is stalked by knuckleheads with long-range lenses, and then is given truckloads of disposable income, the end result can be a human being who is simply a shell, a hologram of who they once were. They are now creatures consumed by an unrelenting emptiness that nothing will fill.

It was my very real fear of becoming this hologram that inspired me to hand my ass back to New York the second my time as a Famous Hollywood Celebrity ended (in other words, *3rd Rock* was canceled). I just wanted to go back to acting in plays, which is what I was doing before I was sidetracked by that damn alien show. I started getting roles I could have only dreamt of when I was a kid, in brilliant plays. I loved it.

Unfortunately, people in Hollywood confuse "having a theater career" with being dead. "*I totally saw a* Dateline *about her last year. How sad is it that they never caught her killer? Hon, we'd like two Cobb salads, please.*" To those who didn't think I was dead, I was labeled "A Has-Been." Which is *totally* different from being dead. I think.

Ah, what the hell did I care? I was doing what I loved! Rehearsing (*drinks after with the cast*), performing (*drinks after with friends*), auditioning (*if I got the role, drinks. If I didn't, more drinks*). Enormous dinners at midnight (*drinksdrinksdrinks*). I gotta tell you, for a while there it was fun, fun, fun. Until my devotion to an incredibly unhealthy lifestyle blossomed out of control, as did my ass—and I became fat, fat, fat.

At the time, however, I was convinced I was simply "bloated," which for some insane reason, I found preferable to "fat." Therefore, when I was occasionally dubbed "a *Fat* Has-Been," I was filled with righteous indignation. "That's *Bloated* Has-Been to you, *National Enquirer!*" Thank God I gracefully graduated from that label era, which I stupidly assumed was as bad as it was gonna get for me. I mean, *a Fat Has-Been*?

Yucky, right?

Turns out, a few brand-spanking-new (and far worse) labels were breathlessly waiting for me just around the corner, absolutely giddy with anticipation.

Up to this point in my life, I had convinced myself that I was a fairly "tough broad." When confronted by anything terrifying (or when simply confronted by anything), all it took was twenty-four hours of weeping on my kitchen floor combined with a bottle of painkillers and a box of red wine, and the next day I'd be good as new.

But because I'm the direct result of generations of people who believed it was a matter of life or death to keep every single flaw or weakness one may have strictly to one's self, I had always found being the object of any press scandal (whether it be true or false) to be profoundly devastating. Not to mention terribly mortifying.

To illustrate what I mean, let's say (and this is purely theoretical) that there was a young lady who hated her thighs. She hid these thighs from everyone, for years. Even with her boyfriend of two years (let's call him Mr. Wonderful), she continually thought of new and creative ways to hide her thighs from him. When naked, she'd either talk as she backed out of the bedroom, "Did I tell you this hilarious story? About Andy being kicked off the plane? Okay, so Andy says . . . wait, I'll tell you after I pee." Or she'd cleverly plant a towel bedside for future coverage. "Gosh, it's freezing. Oh, thank God, here's a towel." This goes on and on. She's thirty-five years old.

Then, one sunny morning as our heroine was

innocently walking her dogs, she happened to walk by a newsstand and was astonished to notice her bathing suit on the cover of a tabloid magazine. *That's funny, I wonder who bought the same suit as me,* she thought to herself, before it hit her. That *was* her bathing suit. And she was, tragically, IN IT.

After pinching herself to make sure this wasn't a nightmare, she grabbed the offending tabloid, and her face drained of all color. There they were. *Her thighs.* Her *secret* thighs, in all their vast and bumpy glory, were being showcased on the cover of the *National Enquirer* under this succinct (yet irresistible) headline "LOOK WHO HAS CELLULITE!"

Certainly at first she probably felt horror and shame and embarrassment. Maybe she even wished she had never been born. She's only human. But really, now that *everyone* (including her second-grade math teacher and that shithead who broke her heart two years ago), oh, my dear baby Jesus, now *every single soul* in the United States who went grocery shopping that week had ALL seen her thighs? Well, then so could Mr. Goddamned Wonderful!

Not that this really happened to anyone I know (*okay,*

it was me), but if it had, I'd certainly hope that the next day I would have been brave enough to rip my clothes off, *turn around*, and fucking *walk* to the bathroom, my thighs proudly sloshing hither and thither. And if Mr. Wonderful didn't like it, well—screw him. (Sadly, I don't think he noticed either way because, like me, he was a total lush.)

It would take a few more years, and one massive disaster, before I would fully understanding the enormity of this. But the exposure of my cheesy thighs was the dawn of understanding. Part one of the most important lesson of my life. Part two would come later. I'll go into greater detail about this, but about five years ago while I was doing a play in London, something truly devastating happened and I underwent a very risky emergency stomach surgery. Months later, when I finally returned to New York, I was sixty pounds lighter, I was also a terrified, raw, unmoored, and very sensitive version of my formerly well-armored self.

Which of course meant that I was in the *perfect* headspace for my brand-new press labels, which were: "SCARY SKINNY!," "ANOREXIC!," or (my personal fave): "LOSING WEIGHT IN A DESPERATE ATTEMPT TO REVIVE HER STALLED CAREER!" Isn't that one just the cutest?

guts

Believe it or not, being savagely attacked in the press with total lies wasn't even the worst part. Suddenly it dawned on me that my very first instinct was to *agree* with the stories, even though I was well aware that every single one of them was categorically untrue.

Oh my God—realization slammed into me, almost knocking me to the floor. *I have spent every single second of my sorry life as a prisoner of what other people think of me.* I had absolutely no concept of myself, not a clue as to who I really was or what my actual feelings were about anything—*because I could only see myself through your eyes.* If you thought I was funny or clever, then I was. If you thought I was pretty or charming, then I was. If you happened to think I was homely, idiotic, annoying, unattractive, talent-free, and worthless? That would've made you perceptive, clever, wise, and bizarrely intuitive.

My mouth went dry. *Oh, my God*, I thought, *that's not only scary—THAT'S FUCKING STUPID.* Finally it permeated my thick idiotic skull: *It's all in my head. If I don't want to care what other people think of me, then I simply don't have to.*

Jesus, I was overwhelmed. Thousands of hours since I was a kid of wishing I was *other*—all wasted. I knew I needed to start accepting that I was me—and I needed to do it pronto—because life, it is short. And the very notion of spending the rest of my life *still* desperately wishing I was anyone but me? Unacceptable.

Coming from a deeply private family, I now know that somewhere along the line I had lost the very important distinction between *privacy* and *secrecy*. And since both brought me nothing but confusion, anxiety, and misery, I've decided to try something new. I'm giving up on trying to control your mind.

Of course, I'd prefer it if you thought I was fabulous; after all, I'm human. I'd prefer it if you thought I was a wonderful actress and a hell of a writer. I'd prefer it if you thought I was funny, and kind. I'd prefer it if *all* men found me charming and beautiful (not just the gays). But if you don't? That's cool, too. (I'd think you were out of your fucking mind, but that's neither here nor there.)

Last year when someone suggested I write a book, I pooh-poohed it at first. But then I started to warm up to the idea. After all, any bonehead can write a book these days. Who's to say mine would suck any worse? Besides, when I took a gander at the overflowing "drunken celebrity memoirs" section, I got the feeling there just might be room for one more poorly written, terribly reviewed, slightly funny, and occasionally moving look at recovery and redemption through the eyes of a giant-Freak-ex-alien-recovering-addict-cellulite-ridden-has-been-actress

If anything, to get a new label. Really. Oh, come on, go ahead. Toss one at me! After Amy, I can take just about anything.

Or who knows? Maybe, just maybe, I'm finally becoming that "tough broad" I always pretended I was.

Therefore, without further ado, I proudly present to you my thighs, in all their vast and bumpy glory.

four

YE OLDE
ELVIS CATNAP

my life changed forever in London on December 4, 2006, when I was thirty-nine years old.

I was doing a play called *Love Song* by John Kolvenbach on the West End with Cillian Murphy, Michael McKean, and Neve Campbell. The director was a lovely and brilliant man named John Crowley, who had dazzled me with his direction of *The Pillowman* on Broadway a few years before. And since I'm bored by most theatrical productions unless I'm in them, this is saying something.

Now, unlike a lot of actors and actresses, I've never understood the whole "I'm too fabulous to audition" thing. If I loved the play and wanted the part, I couldn't wait to get my ass in that room and *earn it.*

I'm lucky that I've always had a fairly solid and sane view of what roles I'm right for. In other words, my agents have never gotten a call from me where I whine, "Why didn't *I* get an audition for Julia Roberts's role in *Runaway Bride*?" Nor have they ever heard, "Why don't *I* have Nicole Kidman's career?" (Not that I haven't wished, believe me.) I'm oh so sorry to say that you'll never see my portrayal of the painfully shy, gimpy Laura in *The Glass Menagerie*, nor will you ever get to hear me say, "O Romeo, Romeo! Wherefore art thou, Romeo?"

I'm certainly not right for every role, but when I am, I *really* am. Take Sally in *3rd Rock*, for example. I was being sent every single funny television script (this is back when they actually made television comedies, before *The Bachelor* and *Wife Swap* ruined everything.) Anytime a show called for a funny girl, I'd audition for it.

If the role was written for a tiny Jewish spitfire, I kid you not, I'd throw on a dark wig and mortify myself.

When I finally got the script for *3rd Rock* a year after it had first been mentioned to me, I ripped open the envelope eagerly. And to my surprise, I discovered it was way, way better than I ever could have imagined. For the first ten pages the aliens spoke in fluent Spanish (with

subtitles of course) until they realized they had landed off-course and were in Ohio. I laughed my ass off. I
thought this was the most arbitrary, stupid, and brilliant
thing ever. But it was Sally, the weapons expert who lost
a bet and ended up in a woman's body, that I knew belonged to me. *No one else will play this role no matter what.*

I fought my ass off to get that part and went through
a grueling eight auditions for it. I'd leave the room, flush
with certain victory, only to hear my agent say, "They love
you, but they love the idea of Kirstie Alley more." But I'd be
called back, again and again and again. I wasn't just waltz-
ing in from ten minutes away, mind you. A few times I'd
have to fly back from New York. Over and over I'd think,
Okay, now they have *to give it to me!* and I'd hear, "They adore
you, but they're checking Ellen Barkin's availability." Even
after I read for Sally in front of the entire staff of the network with John Lithgow and they all gave the thumbs-up
to cast me . . . the producers made me come in *again!*

They wanted a "private work session" with John and
me first thing in the morning and didn't seem to care that
I had to fly in a *third* time from New York on the red-eye.
Okay, now I was starting to get pissed off. This is *my part,*
you weenies. For Christ's sake, what else do I gotta do to

prove it to you? I was sorely tempted to say, "Oh, fuck off, maybe Queen Latifah's available," but I knew I couldn't. They could make me audition twenty more times and I would, because I *would not be denied*. And thank God (for them), I wasn't.

This all helps me illustrate my point, which admittedly I could've made a bit more succinctly, but who can resist a fun trip down *3rd Rock* Lane? My point is, when I'm right for a role *and* I want the role (unfortunately a fairly rare combo), I'll do anything to get it. Get your mind out of the gutter; *of course* excluding sexual favors! Although, come to think of it, I've never even been confronted with that dilemma. Oh, crap. Here's a little window into my sick brain: now that it's occurred to me that I've never been hit on by some lecherous, revolting studio executive, my first thought is, "Well, what's so wrong with me that I've never been molested in an agent's office? Am I really that ugly?"

Yeah, yeah, yeah, London. I'm getting there. The idea of leaving boring old New York and doing a play in a city I loved sounded thrilling. So, even though it had been a long time since I'd had to audition for a theater role, I couldn't wait to get in there and nail it. (Lest I give you the wrong impression, the combination of perfect role and then actually being *cast* in that role happens—oh, I'm gonna say, about 8 percent of the time. Out of 1,000 percent. Usually I'd end up drunk in a bar, throwing darts at Lisa Kudrow's headshot.)

But somehow I got cast (clearly Kudrow was busy), and I excitedly began to prepare for six months in London. Only thing is, I had that nasty little pill problem to contend with. *Doesn't matter!* I thought to myself. *It's a perfect opportunity to stop, once and for all!*

I had stopped before, many times. Withdrawal is no fun, and if you feel the need for a bit more detail, just watch that scene in *Trainspotting* when Ewan McGregor's mother locks him in his room while he detoxes from heroin. I never saw dead babies crawling on my ceiling, but other than that, Vicodin withdrawal is pretty damn close.

It's awful, horrific, but it's survivable. What I was most terrified of was the tsunami of depression that would crash into me and would continue to crash, over and over for months after. Which is why I couldn't ever *really* stop, once and for all.

But I decided I'd worry about that later.

Later came (*she always does, don't she?*), and immediately upon landing I solved my quandry. I was thrilled and deeply relieved to discover that one can buy codeine *over the counter* in London pharmacies. Codeine is a less intense opiate that is turned into morphine once in your system. But because it's much less powerful than Vicodin, I discovered (after much experimentation) that if I took thirty to forty pills a day, I'd be just fine. I was almost proud of myself. *I'm like the Nancy Drew of painkillers!*

The truth was, I had long ago stopped *getting high* or *feeling great* or even *halfway decent* from painkillers. Now, the sole purpose of taking any derivative of codeine or Vicodin was simply to *feel okay*. Whatever the hell that meant. Or I should say, I took them simply to avoid the dreaded Tsunami of Tsorrow. The only problem with my self-prescribed Rx was that the codeine was mixed in with a bunch of aspirin. Unbeknownst to me, at this time I was already suffering from a gnarly peptic ulcer, and ingesting the equivalent of forty to fifty aspirin pills a day wasn't the wisest move.

Taken by the fistful, for a long time, and combined with alky-hol, they eat away at the lining of your stomach and intestinal wall. Somehow, all throughout the heart-burn, difficulty urinating, bloat, exhaustion, depression, anxiety, and generally feeling awful, never once did it cross my mind that I had an *ulcer*. Ulcers were for stressed-out caffeine addicts, not stressed-out painkiller and red-wine addicts.

As rehearsals began, I was starting to feel much worse than I ever did in the States. But doctors had become people to lie to for painkillers; it never occurred to me to go to one because I felt ill.

Opening night, and we were a smash hit. The place was packed, and the reviews glowing. We stayed up into the wee hours getting trashed and celebrating our awesomeness.

The next night, my intestines ripped open.

I swear. I was at my flat, after the second night's performance, sitting on the loo, when I remember feeling a terrifying rip in my stomach area, and I'm convinced I actually heard a horrible ripping sound. This rip was immediately followed by a hurt so powerful, so all-consuming, that, to escape its clutches, I did what any sane person would do and passed out. I had, of course, been endlessly peeing right before said moment, and I barely had time for this quite heroic and even Schultz-like thought before I plowed headfirst into the white tile: *Uh-oh, I must've really pulled a stomach muscle or someth—*

It occurred to me much later that if I had died then and there (and by all accounts I should have), and assuming of course that it had not only been a slow news day, but that Gwyneth Paltrow had decided to stay home, the front page of one of the trashier UK papers might have looked a little something like the following:

"3rd ROCK"-ER SHOCKER!

US Star Found Rotting!
Once Beloved Ex-Alien Dead

*"It was the worst thing I've ever seen,"
says horrified witness. "She was completely
covered in blood and sick."*

(FULL STORY PAGE 16, JUST PAST HOROSCOPES)

HOLLYWOOD TRAGEDY RIGHT HERE IN THE UK!

Kirstine Johnson, 39, found dead on her loo!

THE ACTRESS, whose success began (and unfortunately ended) with the absurd American television comedy *3rd Rock from the Sun,* had recently arrived in the UK to perform on the West End in a misguided attempt to revive her stalled career. She had just opened in the romantic comedy *Love Song* at the Ambassadors and was staying in a rented flat near King's Road.

The cause of death is still undetermined, but due to her youth, nationality and occupation, it's clearly either a drug overdose, suicide or murder. Rumour has it that the forensic examiner is leaning towards homicide. Fingers crossed!

Whatever the cause, the scene was so troubling that a paramedic was witnessed vomiting as he stumbled from the building. Later, a constable commented that the gruesome scene brought to mind the death of Elvis Presley, another bloated (though obviously *far* more successful) American star, because he also happened to meet his maker whilst on his loo in 1977. "Bless her heart, her poor knickers were still round her ankles," the constable said.

The corpse was discovered by a Mr William Sloane, the building's caretaker. He explained that he was simply responding to neighbours' persistent complaints of a terrible odour. He said he expected to find dirty socks or perhaps a rotting plate of bangers and mash. The very last thing he expected to find was a blood-and-vomit-soaked, B-list actress from the US decomposing next to her toilet.

"My God, man, she was grotty," he said, as he shakily lit a cigarette. "Lord forgive me for speaking ill of the dead, but I never liked that alien programme. The wife always fancied 'er, but I always thought she was butters. 'Sides, I never could tell 'er apart from that chubby lass from *Cheers*." ∎

guts

Yet another thing nobody tells you—writing your own faux-bituary is quite enjoyable. I recommend it, especially to those of you with a yen for overdosing.

Let's get back to the stuff that actually happened, like the Rip.

I groggily woke up from my Elvis catnap hours later, having no clue as to where the hell I was. *Whose red bathroom is this?* For the longest time I was just stumped.

Then an overpowering smell of copper.

What the fuck?

Blood? Eww, gross.

Since no one else was there, I assumed that the blood was mine. I had clearly puked blood everywhere, as if in a passionate frenzy. That's when I got an inkling that something very, very bad had happened to me. *Uh-oh.*

I tried to sit up.

A venomous pain walloped me with such a supernatural force that I was slammed back into the tile. *Oh, Jesus, oh my God.* I began to cry the silent wail of a four-year-old who's just had her hand slammed in the car door. The silent cry that threatens to turn into a scream at any second. A pre-cry, I guess you'd call it. A cry that's far, far worse than a cry.

I've felt pain before in my life, real pain, but this was my first introduction to *sheer agony*. And it did not go well. I immediately wished for death, just to escape it. If I had had a gun at that moment, I would've used it without hesitation. The only sane thing I could think of was *Call someone, maybe they'll have a gun. Or a machete.* I'd even be happy with a butter knife.

For the first time in my entire life, I had no idea what to do. I was lost, deep in a terrifying dark forest of torment, and I hadn't a clue as to how to get myself out.

Never had I felt more totally, utterly *alone* than I did at that moment, in the early-morning hours of that cold December day in my rented flat on Cadogan Square. Well, up until that day, that is. I was about to become very intimate friends with *alone*.

I began silently praying, *Get to the phone, just get to the phone, everything will be all right if you can just get to your stupid cell phone.* All while screaming my open-mouthed silent cry. It was almost as if giving my pain a sound would've been disrespectful to it. Or awaken it further.

"*Ohhhhh,*" I said softly as an ice pick rammed into my side. I realized the pain was actually getting worse. It was this pulsating, living thing that seemed to emanate from just under my left rib cage.

Think, you dumb fuck. Where's your stupid phone?

Just then I remembered my habit of dumping everything on the bed of the tiny guest room when I got home with a carefree *Oh, I'll deal later, I gotta open the wine to let it breathe*, which no alcoholic would ever do.

Even though my flat wasn't big, it sure felt pretty enormous when seen from an inch off the floor. Every time I'd move even slightly, a thousand knives instantly plunged into my stomach. I found the tiniest bit of relief in "child's pose," which I soon discovered is not a speedy form of travel. But what choice did I have? There I was, inching along like an exhausted turtle, covered in blood and vomit, sweat pouring down my face, sobbing like a four-year-old, completely committed to the fact that if I was gonna die, I was damn well gonna do it next to my goddamn phone.

I have no idea how long it took me, but my reasonable estimate is an hour. When I finally reached my coat (which I had taken off mere hours before, when I had been a virgin to real pain, blissfully innocent of my coming fate), I yanked it off the bed, found my phone in a pocket, and shakily dialed 999. Eerily, just a few days before, back when I was the old me, someone in rehearsals had mentioned that in the UK their 911 is 999.

When the operator answered, I discovered I couldn't speak. I mean, I *tried* to talk, but I couldn't. Later I would learn that during my Elvis catnap my perforated tummy had leaked out my stomach contents, which had filled up my body, preventing my diaphragm from being able to move. But at the time I had no idea why I couldn't make a sound. I'm fairly certain that I wouldn't have felt better if I *had* known, but it was terrifying just the same. *What the fuck is wrong with me?!*

I must have managed to finally somehow gasp out something because I passed out again and the next thing I knew, my intercom was buzzing. As I slowly inched toward it (thankfully only a few turtle crawls away), I realized I was wearing a vomit-soaked tank top and bloody sweatpants. Not my usual outfit when welcoming the cavalry. Then, with one heroic movement, I used the last of my strength to reach the buzzer—*agony*—and press.

I unlocked the door and slumped down into a puddle next to it. *Thank God, I did it, help is here.* Unfortunately, any relief I felt at being rescued turned immediately to disappointment when I clapped eyes on my saviors, two small men radiating frustration and annoyance. Much later, I would find out that my call had come in at the very end of their shift. But at the time, all I knew was that I had clearly done something terrible to them, and all I could do was gasp out a pathetic "I'm so sorry."

I'll never forget the expression on their faces when they caught their breath and really looked down at me. It was total, absolute revulsion.

Wait a second, hold on. Could it be possible I was the grossest thing they'd *ever* seen? At least in America we have people who are so obese they haven't gotten out of bed in ten years and need a crane to get to the hospital. In America, a sobbing B-list actress stewing in her own juices would at the very *least* be asked for her autograph. Then she'd be quickly filmed with a cell phone. People would view the shaky footage of the very worst moment of my entire life, and they'd feel just terrible for me, while secretly e-mailing it to their friends to gross them out, and eventually I'd get my very own *E! True Hollywood Story*, where I'd alternate between being totally hilarious and weeping with shame, and the ratings would be so high I'd get my own reality show and I'd finally be *back on top!!! USA! USA!*

I digress, get over it. Anyway, I guess I convinced them that I wasn't some crazy, suicidal drunk—ha ha, fooled ya—and that something might actually be seriously wrong with me. Even in my pain I marveled at how these curmudgeons did their jobs every day, when clearly they were far better suited for jobs as meter maids or prison guards. I thought it was terribly rude to judge someone who, even though she looks as if she's an extra from the set of a horror film, is still hotter than either of you.

My flat was on the fifth floor, and I pensively waited for them to give me some painkillers and load me on the stretcher. Except they did neither. It soon became clear that they expected me to *walk* to the exquisitely slow, miniature elevator, which was obviously built at some point during the Elizabethan era. They then expected me to *stand up* in this rickety, minuscule contraption for four minutes, the length of time I knew it would take to deliver me to the first floor.

Which was absolutely out of the question. An impossibility. But as I looked up at them from my knees, my face caked with tears and blood, into eyes that showed me no pity, I realized that's precisely what I was going to do. *No, no, no, oh my dear God . . .*

"Come on, miss, up, up, up, you go. Cheers, yeah, right, up on your feet, that's right, I'm sure it's right painful, here we go. . . . Well, you're going to have to, no two ways about it. Miss, your screaming isn't helping matters. . . . Keep on, there you are, almost. Right. Yes, yes, a few more steps. And here's the lift. Just get on the lift, miss. And here we are. Now that wasn't worth all the fuss, was it?"

Imagine walking completely bent over, like an upside-down *L*. Imagine smelling what I suppose a decomposing corpse must smell like, and then picture being crammed into a tiny, airless moving closet with two people who are clearly already revolted by you. Imagine all of this while being in the most pain a human can bear while remaining conscious.

Finally the elevator door opened, fresh air whooshed in, and for one brief and glorious moment the three of us experienced exquisite relief. I learned one new thing on the elevator ride from hell—if you smell so bad that you actually gross *yourself* out—man, *you stink.*

Much, much later, when I first recalled these men and their awful carelessness and lack of empathy, thoughts of the elevator ride instantly filled me with an evil glee. I guess *Vengeance via Olfactory* is better than nothing.

Eventually with a crisp yet reluctant manner (which okay, *that* I get . . . no one wants to wear someone else's dinner home to the missus), one of them lifted me up and heaved me into the arms of the other guy in the ambulance. Or lorry or trolley or tippy or proggy or foggy or pram or whatever cloyingly adorable fucking name they use. *I wonder what they call a stretcher, because I sure as hell could've used one earlier.* Then they strapped me into what, in my insanity, looked like a booth at Bob's Big Boy. It was probably a bed or something, but what are you gonna do, get all James Frey on my ass? It's my stupid story, I say it was a booth.

After they seat-belted the Big Girl to her Big Boy booth, they proceeded to drive me with exquisite care "to 'ospital." (They don't say "the hospital." They say "'ospital." Don't ask me why, I'm from a country that believes in dentists and ice cubes.)

As we made our way through the cobblestoned streets

guts

of London, my vicious saviors were oh so careful not to miss a single pothole or red light. I didn't even rate that cool *weee-waaaaaw, weee-waaaaaw, weee-waaaaaw* sound.

Much later I'd have to take a cab *to 'ospital* for checkups, and I couldn't believe it took exactly six minutes. I'm convinced that (like a New York cabbie with an unsuspecting tourist) these fuckers took the scenic route. I hoarsely begged them for something to ease my agony. How odd to actually *mean* it, for once. They gave me the gas they told me they give to women about to give birth, which helped not even a little. (But then, my tolerance was so high at this point, I don't think an elephant tranquilizer would've made a dent.)

The next while was a blur—getting to the hospital, being forced to wait endlessly until someone decided to help me. I was in a little curtained-off area of the emergency room, lying on a cot with my knees up to my chin, beyond freezing and just horrified to realize that the agony was getting far worse with each passing moment. It was the kind of pain none of their occasional shots of morphine seemed capable of wrangling.

Oh, the hilarity. Here I am, a gal who's laid waste to

miles and miles of Vicodin. Now when I truly needed it, it was rendered useless? I mean, that's fucked-up, even for you, Satan.

I wondered if pain itself could kill. I tried desperately to concentrate on something happy or pretty, but some asshole was screaming so fucking *loudly* in the ER I couldn't even think.

It was only when a nurse angrily tossed open my curtain and shouted, "Miss, do stop screaming, as you're disturbing the other patients!" did I understand that the constant, earsplitting screams were my own. Later, when thinking about those awful hours—and trust me, I do so as rarely as possible—I can't believe that I was in such terrible straits and clearly so close to death, yet no one gave a shit about me. Least of all me. Never once did it cross my mind to demand to be treated better. Or to scream at the paramedics to bring up a "stretchie" or to *at least* drive the speed limit. Or to karate-chop that rude twat of a nurse's head off.

But in the darkest part of my heart, I'd always known this day would come. I was simply reaping what I had sown, getting exactly what I deserved. So there I lay, the ugliest American, imprisoned in the politest ER in all of

guts

London, a creature of my own making—a now silently screaming, sweating, freezing, smelly, and very, very lonely turtle.

At some point it dawned on me that I might actually be in big, big trouble. The thought was immediately followed by the staggering realization that despite years of slowly killing myself, all I wanted, with more passion and ferocity than I'd ever wanted anything else in my entire life, was to *live*.

five

THE ENGLISH
PATIENT

when people say they simply don't understand how a person could keep using drugs or alcohol even after they've started to lose their job, their friends, their family, their health, I give them this chilling example:

After spending a good hour sequestered in my own curtained-off hell in the ER, the shots they consistently gave me must've finally started working, because I felt oh-so-slightly better. By that, I mean the level of agony had been dialed down from a twelve to a ten, and my screams had died down to very loud moans. Finally, my curtain was drawn back by a nurse endowed with an enormous bosom and a substantial mustache. She was very sweet, as all women with excessive facial hair seem to be, and she cheerfully began the lengthy process of admitting me to the hospital. She asked no-brainers like name, age, race, etc.

She then asked me about my health.

"Do you drink caffeine?"

"Not much." (True.)

"Do you smoke?"

"A little." (A lot.)

"Do you drink?"

"Not excessively." (Not counting the two bottles of wine I suck back a night.)

"Do you do drugs?"

"No." (More than you could even begin to imagine, pretty lady.)

There I was, in sheer agony and probably quite close to dying, yet I lied instantly. Even though the truth very possibly could have saved my life. This is the hardest part for knitters or golfers to comprehend. Because if this woman had said to me right then, "I can guarantee you that *all* of your pain will go away this instant if you tell me the truth right now," I *still* would have lied. Without question.

That's how strong He is. When He's got His evil talons

in you, you don't care. You will lie to protect Him, no matter what happens. He's your most devoted better half, your longtime lover. He's adoring and reliable and He's never let you down. It's certainly not His fault that He's killing you. Like a battered wife, you take Him back even though He just knocked out your two front teeth. You lie to your weeping mother even though He's convinced you to steal the painkillers she actually *needs* after a knee-replacement surgery. You will die protecting Him, no matter what.

Because no one will ever, ever love you as much as He does.

I'll never forget the first time I met Him. It was about fifteen years ago in Los Angeles, and I was deep in the throes of navigating the truly terrifying waters of overnight fame. I was also suffering my first-ever migraine. (Real, by the way. The fake ones came later.) My boyfriend at the time took me to the emergency room of Cedars-Sinai, and about two minutes after the nurse injected Him (in this case, He was morphine) into my ass, I distinctly remember saying to myself, *Holy shit, this is the answer!*

Suddenly, I wasn't depressed or anxious for the first time in years. I can't begin to express the vast sensation of relief that coursed through me. I felt good and confident and at peace. I was *me*, only much, much better. I even signed autographs and posed for pictures on the way out, much to the amusement of my boyfriend. *Go ahead and laugh it up, buddy. 'Cause my heart no longer belongs to you.*

Of course, like any good love story, it took many years for us to finally give in and admit our feelings for each other. I kept Him at bay for as long as I could. But He was so *persistent*. We'd see each other, break up, then I'd give in again, then dump Him. His given name was Opiate, but He went by many aliases. (Which should have been my first red flag.) I didn't care what name He went by, I'd have known Him anywhere. He was known as Codeine, Heroin, Fioricet with Codeine, Vicodin, Hydrocodone, Hycodan, Darvocet, Percocet, and my personal favorite, Morphine, to name just a few. I adored them all, but I must say I'm *exceedingly* grateful I never ingested either Heroin (a powerful derivative of the opiate), or his rascally, good-for-nothing cousin OxyContin. Because I know with absolute certainty that, if I had, I'd be deader than a doornail. Doorknob? Whatever, I'd be dead.

All opiates, also known as painkillers, are derived

from opium, which is extracted from the seeds of the poppy flower. Scientists have, of course, created imitators, but I've never been a fan. It's kind of like your boyfriend being suddenly replaced by a robotic replica. (Oh my God, after all these years, it just occurred to me that when Dorothy was surrounded by all those poppy flowers, she wasn't being forced to fall asleep, she was just having a good, old-fashioned heroin nod. Not very wicked of the ol' witch, if you ask me.)

Back to my point. I've talked to many people about painkillers, both drug addicts and the knitting/love/work addicted. This is a purely unscientific study, but I've discovered that drug addicts and the knitters have completely different experiences when they take painkillers. Almost all of the knitters said they had pretty much the same experience. The drugs made them feel kind of nice for a bit and helped relieve their pain, but they mostly just experienced itchy skin, constipation, and nausea. Most of them said that they were happy and relieved to stop taking the pills. There were a few who admitted they liked to save one or two to have later with margaritas. I'll be seeing you in a church basement at some point in the next few years. But have fun while you can, "knitter."

Now, the reaction of the drug addict's brain is just slightly different. It goes a little something like *Yes! Yes! Thank you!!!! This is what I've been waiting for all these years. I finally feel normal, I finally feel happy! MORE MORE MORE MORE MORE MORE . . .*

And that's what makes me suspect that addiction might just have a little something to do with people's different brain chemistries and isn't just because we're lazy, pleasure-seeking narcissists, hell-bent on ruining our lives. The addicts instantaneously and utterly lose their fucking minds, and I can say from experience that their minds aren't exactly in a hurry to be found. These people suddenly become just like that guy in your neighborhood who invests in full-out, life-or-death screaming matches with air. Or that woman who insists on wearing six-inch platform heels to work every day and wonders why she's always in such a shitty mood. Or that construction worker who's convinced that because he screams "I love pussy from outer space!" at me, I'll immediately drop my dog leash and groceries and run toward him as fast as I can, ripping my clothes off on the way.

---

guts

The biggest problem with being crazy is that you don't *know* you're crazy. So, while being asked those questions as I was being admitted to that hospital, I thought nothing of lying, of quickly giving the answers a "normal" person would give. (A normal person with a machete in her tumtum, that is.) I was an expert at both lying and pretending to be normal, I'd been doing both for years. And I most definitely wasn't crazy. Not one bit.

Soon afterward, it seemed I'd finally worn out my welcome in the ER and was wheeled to the X-ray room. At first I was relieved, thinking I was one step closer to getting that pill or shot or whatever would cure me (along with a boatload of painkillers with three refills), so I could leave this hellhole and go home, where I could scream as loud as I wanted to into my pillow. The surly technician, who had clearly excelled at the same school of bedside manners as the ER nurse and the paramedics, refused to believe that it was physically impossible for me to bring my knees down from my chin. He kept insisting, saying it was the only way to X-ray my stomach area, and I kept telling him, "No, no, please, no, I can't do it, I swear."

But he'd obviously gotten wind of what a loud asshole I'd been in the emergency room because he wasn't putting up with my nonsense. In a decisive move that would have made Heinrich Himmler weep with pride, he cut to the chase and simply *yanked* my legs down with of all his evil might.

Which took me to a place way beyond pain. I can't believe I didn't pass out again, but that would've been a gift. And people like me don't deserve gifts.

As he took the X-rays, he kept ordering me to stop shivering, as though I were doing it just to be difficult. But I couldn't help it. I was constantly and violently shuddering due to the fact that not only was the drafty, old hospital as warm and cozy as a meat locker, but all I had to keep me warm was my revolting tank top and putrid sweatpants. I'm also quite sure that I was very close to going into shock. He finally took pity on me and kindly tossed me a thin hand towel, which I covered my face with so he wouldn't see me cry.

I lay on that cold, black slab and immediately reverted to when I was a little girl, that baffling time in my life when I tried so hard to be good, yet somehow always mysteriously failed. *If I was still and wasn't loud and screamed only inside my head, then would my mommy come?*

Finally, the torture was done, for now.

guts

It was then that I began some eternal journey, with no explanation, somewhere else deep into the bowels of the cavernous, old hospital. Even though my recent life had clearly been awful in many ways, I had always been proudly self-reliant, independent, and 100 percent self-sufficient. Probably to a fault.

Yet, in the space of a few hours, I'd been utterly decimated. All those years of bravado crushed to dust. So easily. I watched it all fly away, helpless to stop it.

What remained was a powerless, nameless creature being wheeled through a busy hospital on a gurney, helplessly obligated to the bored gentleman assigned to push me. I was no longer a person, I was now something people gave pitying glances to or gossiped over in the elevator, something that no longer had a name, a voice, ears, arms, or legs.

I now was a *patient*.

And let me just say that if I knew then what was about to happen to me, you better fucking *believe* I would've rolled right off that lolly and turtle-crawled my ass all the way back to New York City.

six

DYING IS EASY,
LIVING IS HARD

don't ask me how my memory of these events is so lucid when I can't remember my best friend's birthday, what I ate for breakfast, or even what time my weekly shrink appointment is. However, for some reason almost every unfortunate moment, from waking up in my gore-splattered bathroom to the day I finally checked out of the hospital two months later, is burned into my memory. It used to baffle me because I'm renowned for my flakiness, yet *this nightmare* is what I choose to retain? But now I understand. How could something that changed your life *not* be seared into your memory?

I remember lying on a gurney in some sort of ward crammed with people. I was terribly disappointed to

119

discover that, other than being overcrowded, this ward bore zero resemblance to the London hospital wards as described by Charles Dickens. This was white, sterile, and cold, as if designed by Stanley Kubrick's tacky younger brother, Jim Bob.

The fantastic news was that the thirtieth shot of morphine had finally kicked in about five minutes earlier and I was feeling better. I was cured! I could just get a prescription for six hundred painkillers with four refills and be sent on my merry way! That thought made me feel close to excellent.

Since I was then able to remove my knees from my chin and stand for ten seconds at a time, they changed me into a lovely white hospital gown (and by lovely I mean in relation to what I'd previously been wearing). They removed my vomit-hardened sweatpants ("Yes, I'm positive, Nurse. Please just throw them away. I mean, unless *you* want 'em?") and emptied out my pockets. When they moved away to bring over the scale, I spotted my cell phone (the one I had bought when I was the other Kristen), and something told me to grab it and hide it. Having a cell phone there might be completely fine, but because I'm a lying, pill-popping lush, it's hardwired into my brain to assume that anything I want or need isn't allowed and therefore must be hidden. To this day, even if I'm taking an innocent aspirin, I have to resist the urge to exclaim, "Wow, look at the squirrel!" and quickly pop it into my mouth when backs are turned.

The phone made it under my pillow just as they came over to weigh me. The nurse kindly offered to translate my weight from stone to pounds, without even being asked. "That would have you at just over 190 US pounds, dear!" (One hundred and ninety pounds! Holy crap, that's not just bloated! I'm a fatfatfatty-kins.) But because I was ensconced in my morphine bubble, I found it funny instead of deeply depressing. *Fatty.*

I was put back in my bed and waited until they left. I grabbed the phone. It was too early to call anyone in the United States, so I called the stage manager to tell him I wasn't going to come in today. He seemed rather alarmed when I told him what had happened, but I assured him, "Malcolm, relax. I'm as tough as they come. I've never missed a show before in my life. I've even gone on with the flu." This is true. I would run to the wings, vomit, and return right back to the show. Hey, just because I'm addicted to painkillers doesn't mean I'm a pussy.

"Okay, you worrywart, I'll call you as soon as I know anything, but I'm positive I just pulled a stomach muscle or something, and I'll be good as new tomorrow!" Now that I think back on it, I was bizarrely chipper. He must have thought I had actually lost my mind. (That is, if he hadn't already.) I mean, who the hell would be bubbly at a hospital at a time like this?

A drug addict who's high, that's who.

I don't know how long I snuggled into my downy-soft morphine duvet, but suddenly the mood in the ward shifted. *Something's happening,* I thought to myself, just as a team of about ten impossibly serious-looking people rounded the corner. It took an embarrassingly long time for me to realize that they were coming toward me. Which was baffling, until I realized that the hospital must have finally realized that "Ivana Humpalot" was in their very hospital and had quickly assembled an impressive-looking welcoming committee to apologize for their previous unpleasantness. I smiled forgivingly.

The group took formation around my bed, a well-practiced ballet designed to impress. A few of them looked as if they had just started grade school. Not one of them looked older than twenty-three. That is, with the notable exception of their leader. As he walked toward me, I have this fuzzy and hopefully untrue memory of my jaw dropping open. (Oh, dear God, please tell me I shut it at some point.) He reached out his gorgeous hand to shake mine and introduced himself. This man was so elegant, darkly stunning, and breathtakingly handsome, I instantly thought of one of those impossibly perfect heroes found only in Danielle Steel novels my sister used to beg me to read aloud. *"His icy eyes focused on her pillowy lips and suddenly she knew she was his, forever . . ."* We could easily spend an entire Saturday doing this, laughing until our faces hurt.

Lost in this memory, I slowly realized *his* pillowy lips were moving. *Whoopsies, he's talking.* Seeing as I was committed to making our relationship work, I decided to listen to his soft-yet-commanding voice. I missed the beginning, and most of it was medical lingo that flew over my addled mind, but I'll give you the gist.

". . . ulcer for quite a long time. I'm surprised you haven't experienced more discomfort before this. Regardless, this has caused an erosion of the gastrointestinal wall, which has led to your intestinal content spilling into your abdominal cavity. We call this acute peritonitis, which is the reason for the sudden onset of your intense abdominal pain. To be blunt, Ms. Johnston, you could die at any moment."

My smile faltered. This wasn't at *all* what I expected. *And where's the cheese plate?*

"We must perform a very risky surgery, called a gastrectomy, to fix this. We are rushing you ahead of all other patients. We will try to fix this problem with laproscopic surgery, meaning, through five incisions around your stomach. However, there is a very good chance this won't work, and then we'll have to cut you open with a rather large incision across your stomach. Obviously, we'd like to avoid that if we can, for obvious reasons."

Obviously. I nodded in total agreement. We'd rather avoid an enormous, disfiguring scar across the tummy, if at all possible.

"Unfortunately, your X-rays are, to say the least, very confusing, so we'll have to make some difficult choices whilst you're in surgery. I want to be very clear that anything could happen, really. We need your signature that gives us permission to make the appropriate judgment call."

guts

He then looked around at his minions, who immediately murmured words of agreement. "Ms. Johnston, I suggest you let your loved ones know."

I smiled dreamily at him. "Okay, Doctor. You do what you gotta do."

He leaned forward and looked at me seriously. "Do you have any questions?"

"Ummmm . . . Yep, no, I'm good."

This seemed to disappoint him. But what was I supposed to do? Start screaming, *"Noooo! I want to live!!!"*? I just didn't have it in me. He held forward something to sign, and I eagerly scribbled the signature of a drunken toddler. His face remained blank. "Yes. Well, Ms. Johnston. See you very soon."

"Okay, bye-bye." I'm pretty sure I waved. I hope to *God* I didn't wink.

And with a whoosh, they were gone. I sighed, in love. I wondered if I looked hot. I'm pretty sure not, because when I coyly reached up to fluff my hair, I found it to be rock hard with remnants of last evening's detritus. Aww, puke-mousse. Bummer.

All was quiet. I looked around the packed ward and

it was then that I realized that I was the only one alone. Well, other than for my boyfriend Mr. Morphine, that is. Who was a *total* sweetheart for being here, but was (no offense) not so good at getting me water, saying comforting things, or wiping my brow.

My attention was caught by the grief-stricken face of an ancient lady who was holding the paper-thin hand of an equally ancient and clearly almost-dead lady in the corner. Somehow, I knew they were sisters and were all each other had, their whole lives, and that once the sick one died (in two days), the other would follow within the month, of a broken heart.

Thankfully, the Indian family to my left distracted me from that total bummer. These people were fascinating because even though the giggling little boy in the hospital gown had obviously been completely cured of whatever had once ailed him, they were clearly in no rush to leave. They were clearly so happy to be together. The loud uncle in the Cosby sweater had everyone laughing, and a little birdie told me *he* was no stranger to Jesus Juice.

He quickly became annoying to Mr. Morphine, so I turned my head to the bed to my right, where an attractive middle-aged (wait, oh my God, am I middle-aged?)

blond woman was being comforted by her husband. She had clearly eaten something bad, which in London, where even an apple smells like beef stew, isn't exactly a shocker. I cleverly deduced that they were German tourists because he was wearing a man-purse and clogs. The fact that they were speaking German was also helpful. (Well, it could have been Austrian, Swedish, or even Russian, but I'm an American, we don't need to know such things.)

Wherever they were from, I wondered if she knew how lucky she was to have someone who, despite his unfortunate taste in accessories, was willing to gently rub her back even while she vomited bile into a bowl. He suddenly looked sharply up at me, and instead of pretending I hadn't been staring, I smiled. He was not charmed, so I looked away. *Oh! I get it* . . . he must've thought that because no one was with me, I was one of those creepy, friendless people. Someone so awful that no one would comfort her, even on her deathbed. I was sorely tempted to explain that my longtime lover *was* here, thank you very much, but something told me he wouldn't understand. How could he, when even I didn't?

I realized I was still clutching my cell phone, and after

about forty minutes of trying very, very hard to figure out what time it would be in New York (math and morphine are not friends), I called my oldest friend in the world, Jackie. The second I heard her voice, I burst into tears.

Because I could hear her going "What? Oh, my God, Kris, what is it?" I pulled myself together, took a shallow breath, wiped my tears with one of the tiny sheets of sandpaper conveniently located in a box next to the bed, and said, "Listen, Jack. Don't panic, okay? But I'm in this hospital in London, and apparently my stomach blew up, and they're going to operate on me and I called you because I wanted yours to be the last voice I ever hear." (A little known fact is that acting like a drama queen upon one's deathbed is not only acceptable, it's encouraged.)

You gotta know Jackie. This information was like setting an atom bomb off in her brain. *"What?????"* she screamed. *"What are you talking about!!!!!"* The entire ward stopped and looked over, except the "funny" uncle, who was clearly in the middle of a punch line and kept right on going (good man, I would have done the same myself).

I glanced smugly at the German man. *See? I'm not*

creepy. I have a friend in New York who screams into the phone at the mere mention of my demise! But he was ignoring me.

I did my best to explain to Jackie what the doctor had said, and when she finally calmed down, she told me about this friend of a friend of hers who had the *exact* same surgery, and he was *fine.*

Much later, she would admit that the guy had burned a hole in his intestines from doing too much coke and he wasn't fine at all. He was, in fact, dead.

"Whew," I told her.

"What do they think caused it?"

Don't even pause. Go with . . . "Cigarettes, I guess."

"Wow, really?"

"Well, that's what the surgeon thinks. I mean, what *else* could it be?"

Jackie, so sweet and trusting, was completely unaware of my torrid romance with M. She fell for it hook, line, and sinker. The tiniest squirt of guilt and it was gone.

Much later, I'd find out that she, along with my closest friends Laura, Joe, Andy, and John, had all suspected that I had a serious problem for the last few years. They had all wanted to say something, and a few of them had kind of danced around it, but it seems as though I had surreptitiously forced all of them to sign some sort of ironclad, unbreakable contract, which could be summed up thusly:

"If you ever attempt to discuss the elephant in the room, Kristen's head will explode and you will be held responsible for her death and spend the rest of your life in a Siberian work prison."

Anyone who's ever loved a drug addict or alcoholic knows how impossibly difficult it is to address it with us. It doesn't help matters that while protecting our disease, most of us are incredibly crafty, manipulative, demanding, and just plain old scary. *Or maybe that's just me?*

Let's just say I wouldn't have been terribly receptive to their concerns, and they knew it. In fact, I would've most likely had a full-scale meltdown that rivaled Chernobyl. But let's not get ahead of ourselves. Back then, unbeknownst to me, I was spending my last few weeks in my beloved Schultz-ville, an adorable, quaint, old village where Jackie thinks I'm perfectly healthy except sometimes I drink too much, and where cigarettes make your stomach blow up.

"Jackie, please tell me I'm full of shit."

guts

"Umm, okay. You're full of shit."

"For once, you'd be right."

This is why I love Jackie. Toss her a crappy joke like that and she'll still give me one of her gut laughs, my favorite sound in the whole world.

(Time lost here in Morphine cuddle.)

Suddenly, my bed seemed to crash-land in some sort of anteroom outside the "operating theater." Which sounds much more exciting than "operating room." It made me feel as though an audience were going to *ooh* and *aah* at every deft move my swarthy surgeon made. I hoped he'd have a good show today.

This thought sent a shiver of terror down my spine, and as I waited and waited (for the audience to find their seats?), I suddenly knew, beyond the shadow of a doubt, that the anesthesia wouldn't work properly and I would be one of those rare people who feel everything during the entire surgery, yet can't say anything. I remember truly believing this would happen, with every fiber of my being. Panic began to overwhelm me. I suddenly realized they must've told Mr. Morphine he had to stay in the waiting room. *Oh, no . . .*

Just then, an older man in scrubs walked into the

anteroom to grab a vial of something. As he turned to go back onstage, he saw me lying there. "Well, hello *you!*" he said, as if we had bumped into each other whilst having tea at the Dorchester.

"Are you a doctor?"

He must have picked up on my abject terror and walked over to me. "Why, yes. I'm Dr. Blankety-Blank. I've just finished a small operation, and now I'm helping them prepare yours. Why do you ask, darling?"

I love how in England a complete stranger can call you "darling" and somehow you're charmed and flattered, even in the scariest moment of your life. I began to weep like a little girl as I told him I was certain I'd be awake during the operation.

He then did one of the kindest things anyone has ever done for me (up until then, that is). He gave the object he'd come in for to a passing ghostlike nurse, took his gloves off, and held my hand. His was large with salt-and-pepper hair on his knuckles. His grip was strong and reassuring. I began to calm down as I let his confidence pour into me. I'd no idea how desperately I needed it, the simple, caring touch of another human being.

Even though his name was immediately lost to me

and I never saw him again, I'll never forget what he did as long as I live. He stood there with me for a long, long time, soothing me. Then he removed the last of my fears by saying the magic words: "Don't worry, love, you won't remember a thing."

After all, that pretty much described my average evening. Some ghosts came in then to take me, and he had to let go of my hand. As I was pulled into the theater, I'm almost certain I heard him say, *"Break a leg, darling."*

I tried to thank him for his kindness, but at that moment a ghost put a mask on my face. I felt something wet and cold on my belly just as I saw my gorgeous surgeon, and suddenly I realized I needed to tell him something impor . . .

seven

BLINK

. . . and I was someplace else now, in a hallway full of beeping machines and someone saying my name. I wanted to tell my surgeon something but I couldn't see him.

Blink. I was immediately somewhere else, a curtain drawn around me, and I looked to my left and saw my English friend Joanna. *How the hell did she get here? I didn't call her.* She appeared upset. I tried to say, *What's wrong?*—but something was in my throat.

Blink. Joanna was gone.

Blink. This time Malcolm, my stage manager from the play, was there. *Hey, Malcolm!* But he was busy arguing with a harried-looking Asian man in scrubs. *This should be fun. Nothing better than a good Malcolm scrap.*

"At least three weeks," the man said.

"Oh, dear God," Malcolm said as he slumped into a chair. Well, that wasn't entertaining one bit. I was tempted to blink again, but my mouth was drier than it had ever been before and I was suddenly overwhelmed with a desperate need for water.

I tried to talk, but that weird thing was still in my throat.

"Wat . . . ," I croaked, and that tiny syllable was all it took for Malcolm to turn into Shirley MacLaine from *Terms of Endearment.*

"My God, man, *hurry!* Can't you *see* she needs water?"

The Asian man said, "I'm sorry, sir, I'm not allowed."

If I could've moved my diaphragm, I would've gasped in amazement. *Oh, no you di'int!* You don't ever tell Malcolm no. Malcolm is a tall, elegant, imposing man with a wonderful laugh who would be as comfortable on a yacht as he would in the merchant marine. He's the kind of gentleman who could run six blocks to catch a purse snatcher without losing the ash on his cigarette.

He drew himself up to his almost-seven-foot glory, and with an icy voice that could scare the crap out of the queen mum's corgis, he said, "Young man, either you get her a cup of water, *imm-edjate-ley*, or I shall."

"Well . . . I'm not supposed to, but . . ." *Do it! Do it, man, if you want to live!* "I suppose she could have a few ice chips."

At the word *ice* I perked up. Ice turns into water, doesn't it?

"*Well?*" Malcolm said imperiously. The man scurried off, dignity destroyed but balls intact.

Malcolm winked at me and sat back down. "There there, dear," he said as he awkwardly petted my foot. I'm not sure he'd ever actually touched anyone before. "The ice will be here before you know it."

Thank you, you don't have to touch me anymore—

Blink. Malcolm was gone. The very relieved Asian man was offering me a cup of ice chips.

"Hello there, miss. Have a nice nap? I'm Eddie. You're in the ICU, and I'm keeping watch over you tonight."

He held out a Styrofoam cup full of little scrapings of ice, and I almost didn't recognize the trembling hand that slowly reached out to take it from him. My skin was greenish, as if I'd been in prison for a year, and my wrist was shockingly tiny, with pinpricks and IVs everywhere and a medical ID bracelet.

I relished the ice as it drizzled into my mouth, but seriously, *What was in my throat?* Pointing to my throat, I signaled *What?* to Eddie.

He explained (and I paraphrase here) that it was a tube that was draining my stomach hoo-ha out. It started at the surgical site in my tummy, continued from there, and traveled all the way up my throat and through my right nostril, which is where it exited my body. It was attached to a clear pouch that hung with a bunch of other pouches two feet away. The tube was unfortunately transparent, and you do not even want to know the hibbidy-gibbidy craziness I saw move through that tube over the next few days. At the moment, all it was draining was brown stuff, which looked rather harmless.

Eddie was continuing his cheerful explanation of all the tubes and wires I was hooked up to, which got rather boring. Just as I was about to blink, he said the magic word: *morphine.* He saw that it caught my attention, so he went into detail, saying that the enormous catheter jammed into my neck artery (okay, that kills) was how they were getting essential antibiotics and morphine directly into me. *On second thought, it doesn't hurt* that much. . . .

Blink.

Eddie was holding a phone to my ear, saying, "Miss? Wake up, it's your mum. She's anxious to speak to you."

"Ma?" I squawked.

"Oh, sweetie, are you okay?" My eyes welled up at the sound of her voice. I could picture her in her kitchen in Milwaukee, her beloved shar-pei puppies at her feet.

"Oh, I'm fine." (Let me tell you, it's harder than you'd think to sound fine with a tube draining sordid nonsense through your throat.)

"Really? Do you want me to come back?" She had just left London two days ago. I could tell she was crying. I despised making my mother cry. In fact, there might be no worse feeling on earth.

"No!" *She can't come. No matter what, convince her she can't come.*

"Sweetie, are you sure?"

"Yes!" I croaked cruelly, and handed the phone back to Eddie. Otherwise I knew I'd burst into tears, which would not only be painful, but disastrous.

You see, for some reason, ever since I was a kid, it

had always been of the utmost importance to me to convince her, and anyone else dumb enough to love me, that I didn't *need* them. That I wasn't *needy*. I was pathologically obsessed with appearing as *unneedy* as possible.

I can't tell you how many of my past romantic relationships started off with the guy thinking, *This is the coolest, most independent chick ever!* and ended with him shouting, "Why are you sobbing? You said you were cool with us dating other people! You're fucking crazy!"

What they never seemed to grasp was that I wasn't *lying* as much as I was presenting the person *I wished I were*. I can't tell you how many miserable mountain climbs I've been on ("I love mountain climbing!"), or how many endless monologues I've sat through about subjects that meant less than nothing to me ("I'm completely fascinated by chess!"). Thankfully, this unfortunate habit ended when one of my best friends, John Benjamin Hickey, watched in amazement as I earnestly uttered this doozy to some hot guy: "I can't believe it! I'm totally obsessed with fly-fishing, too!"

We laughed our asses off later, but underneath, it made me feel uneasy. I wondered why I felt this need to lie about myself to attract a man. Or why I thought that the real me wasn't nearly enough. So, many years ago, before I even got sober, I managed to stop lying to guys (except about my drug and alcohol consumption). Here's the truth: I hate football, and I will never, ever care about it. Sorry. You enjoy, though.

But one charming quality of mine wasn't as easy to get rid of (in fact, I still grapple with it, although I'm getting better). I staunchly refused to admit that I needed anyone. Especially my mother. I was completely unaware that by simply uttering "No!" to her, my fate was sealed for the next few months. In that second I committed myself to *being alone.* The next time I saw my mother it was four months later, at Family Week at rehab.

I'm still amazed at the choice I made. At that time, I would rather lie alone, hour after hour, day after day, week after week, for almost *two months*, than to have to tell anyone I needed them.

You see, if I needed them, that would mean I was weak, which would mean I was flawed. And *that* would be unacceptable. A fate far worse than death.

I gestured to Eddie to give me more morphine.

"Thank—"

Blink.

eight

I THINK WE'RE
ALONE NOW

a few years ago I saw this documentary about two best friends who had climbed some mountain in Peru together. One of them falls into a deep crevasse, and the other— thinking, *of course he's dead*—cuts the rope connecting him and leaves him. There's just a teeny problem—the guy *wasn't* dead after all! He was just stuck a few miles down in some vast ice cave with a totally shattered body. Not-so-dead guy heroically inches his way back down the mountain, nearly dying of thirst, constantly reinjuring himself, and basically going completely nuts. It takes a week. But he survives.

What struck me the most was that throughout this horrific, endless nightmare, he can't get this totally idiotic pop tune he *hates* out of his mind no matter what he does. He just can't believe he's going to die with this stupid song running through his brain. I sat there in the dark theater, chilled to the bone. Because for weeks, lying in that hospital bed, no matter what I did, I could not get Tiffany's pop song "I Think We're Alone Now" out of my head.

It was the first thing that popped into my head at 6:30 a.m. when the nurses would wake me up to check my vitals. Which was fantastic, since I was desperate to get an early start on another day of pain and boredom. It was the last thing I hummed as I tried (and usually failed) to fall asleep. It occurs to me only now that this song must have become some perverse way of my subconscious expressing the bottomless crevasse of all-encompassing loneliness *I* had fallen into.

Thus, the battle not to feel sorry for myself had begun. This was probably easier for me than for most people because, while growing up, "feeling sorry for ourselves" was treated as a highly undesirable character trait by my parents, especially my father. Therefore, we were trained that "feeling sorry for one's self" was unacceptable, as were any emotional states that didn't resemble "happiness," "contentment," or at the very least "cheerful productivity." If we were bored or upset or even slightly crabby, a nice brisk round of chores was immediately assigned. Nothing makes a kid stop crying faster than cleaning out the garage.

However, one unexpected component made my battle not to feel bad for myself even that much harder. You see, in London, feeling sorry for yourself is looked upon quite differently than it is in the U.S. Instead of a flaw, the Brits seem to find it rather charming. In fact, the worse you feel for yourself, the more the Brits seem to adore you. Of course, they have a darling name for it. It's simply called *poor YOU.*

This is one of the main qualities of the British I will forever adore (comedic brilliance and a profound appreciation for the macabre run a close second). If *any* misery whatsoever were to befall you, whether it be getting caught in the rain or accidentally being tortured in Abu Ghraib for six weeks, there's no difference. Each would be treated equally and you would be greeted with a heartfelt and utterly sincere "Poor *you.*" Sometimes, you'd get a *darling* tacked on, and you already know how I feel about *that* word. Or sometimes (ooooh, it gives me chills just thinking about it), you'd hit the mother lode and get "Poor *you*. Well, I, for one, cannot imagine that play without your performance, darling!"

But it was very near impossible to ignore how I was raised. Besides, I didn't deserve pity, even from myself, because my stupidity had caused this fucking thing. I may have lied to the hairy lady and Jackie, but I knew the truth. While I had been laughing it up in Schultz-ville, all those painkillers had been busy carving out a huge hole in my guts. How dare I even consider asking my friends to drop their lives to come hold my hand when my selfishness alone caused this mess. So, I resisted the urge to feel sorry for myself with all my might. And it worked, for a while. The loneliness was a bit harder to keep at bay.

My loneliness was compounded by the fact that Malcolm had apparently emasculated someone else and I ended up in a private room instead of a ward. Which I was exceedingly grateful for at first, until it became so mind-numbingly boring that when the old man down the hall performed his daily ritual of slowly hobbling by my door, exercising his brand-new hips, it was the highlight of my day.

I think we're alone now. . . .

guts

I had a television, which one could apparently pay sixteen pounds per day to watch, but I couldn't even bear the thought of reaching for the remote attached to it, let alone fishing my credit card out of my enormous purse in the corner. Even if I could get the TV happening, I doubt I could've paid even the slightest attention to it. Despite the good, old-fashioned pain that follows having a chunk of one's intestines removed, there was the joy of a large tube removing tummy blech through my throat and nose. Simply swallowing took a concentrated effort. Not that I *had* any reason to swallow, mind you. My saliva glands had obviously been removed by accident during the operation. I also stoically ignored the powerful current of pain radiating from my neck catheter because that's how Mr. M was consummating our relationship. Although, even *He* was a disappointment because, as every addict knows, drugs are never fun when you actually *need* them. And I needed them badly. I had to fight the urge to be jealous of my intestines.

Another consequence of being an addict is that by now I had many, many friends, but no one who really *knew* me. How could they when I didn't let them? But I got loads of flowers. Lots and lots of flowers. And phone calls. And e-mails. But again, it never occurred to me to ask my friends or family to come over from the U.S. I'm sure if it occurred to *them* to fly over, they quickly said to themselves, "Don't be stupid. She would *hate* that!"

I can't even imagine how different an experience it would have been to have been surrounded by people who loved me. To have felt *worthy* of that kind of love and care. I suddenly thought of the Indian family, and that lucky little boy. No wonder he was laughing.

I, however, was not laughing and couldn't imagine ever laughing again. I never realized how much one uses one's stomach. To sit, stand, breathe, reach, lie down, get back up, walk, talk, everything. I became still as a mummy, petrified to move even a tiny bit, for even clearing my throat would suddenly awaken my newly edited and fragile tummy.

After some time had passed (an hour? a day? five minutes?) I suddenly, oh-so-slightly coughed, which after eight seconds of reverberating agony jolted my memory. *Oh, my God, I completely forgot! I'm a pack-a-day smoker!*

Uh-oh. I was instantly slammed with a brand-new NEED. A kind of NEED only smokers and ex-smokers will understand. It had been two days since I last smoked, and even though it was the first time I'd even thought of it (which shows you how truly distracted I was), it was as if a switch had been turned on and I suddenly wanted to smoke more than I wanted water. Shit. That thought made me crave water, too. Water, cigarette, water, cigarette, need, need, need.

One of the nurses must have finally heard my incessant buzzing (which, by the way, even *I* could hear) and managed to extricate herself from the loud trash-fest she and another nurse were having at the front desk across from my room. I heard her sigh, say something unintelligible to the other nurse, who laughed, and she slowly shuffled in, as if I were this enormous pain in the ass.

Which, I most certainly *was*, but *she* didn't know that yet.

"Wot?" she said through her mouthful of gum.

Jesus, what if I had been dying for fuck's sake? "Umm . . . I . . ."

"Yew in payun?"

After the briefest moment of deciphering, I croaked, "Yes!" (Well, I *was*.)

"Press bu-un, more med-cine."

I looked to where she was pointing, a button near my hand that kind of resembled the buttons on a heating

pad. *Click.* Oh, what a smashing idea. My very own bu-un!
Clickity. Click. Click . . .

"Thank you," I croaked.

She turned away.

"No, no, wait please . . . I really need a cup of water
[*cigarette*]. Or chicken broth [*cigarette*] or even ice chips
[*cigarette*]."

"You can't have noffing till Misser James say."

"Not even ice chips?" I begged.

"Noffing till Misser James say."

And who on earth was this mysterious and all-
powerful Mr. James? *Ooooh!* Maybe he'll be gay, which
would mean we'd instantaneously adore each other.
"Mr. James" *sounded* gay, although in England, where
even straight men wear ascots, it can be difficult to tell.
Also, if he were gay, he might look past the fact that I
stank worse than a vomit-caked bathroom in a frat
house after a toga party. He'd adore me just for being
revolting li'l ol' me. I imagined a lifelong friendship: me,
Mr. James, and his hot boyfriend, Mr. Allastair, arrang-
ing yearly trips to Ibiza, where . . .

Uh-oh, I was losing her.

"Well, where is this Mr. James?"

She looked at me as if I were nuts. Which I most cer-tainly *was*, but *she* didn't know that yet.

"He in *surgery*. Misser James your *surgeon*." Oops. "I can't give you noffing till Misser James *say*."

Okay, I heard you the first time, you nasty wench. Why wouldn't she just call my surgeon "doctor?" I wondered. (I found out later that in the UK, doctors were called "doc-tor" and surgeons were called "mister." Again, ice cubes.)

"Doctah Smyjoes will check on ye t'morr." She started to leave, her duty done.

"Wait, sorry. Who's Dr. Smyjoes? I mean . . . maybe you could call him?"

She gathered the little strength she had left. "He's part of your team, 'ssisting Misser James on your case." At this point, she was so done with me that she almost ran out of the room, shutting the door behind her with finality.

That did it. I finally gave in and burst into baby tears. *Poor ME.*

I think we're alone now, there doesn't seem to be anyone around. . . .

Time passes at a hellish pace when you're not only feeling sorry for yourself but you can't eat, talk, breathe, drink, smoke, read, walk, sit up, or stand. It's just you, you, and more you. Mr. M is busy dealing with intestinal stuff, so He can't help. No one can. I remember looking at the clock on my bedside, which said 13:15 p.m.

Hours passed.

I looked again.

It said 13:18 p.m.

Dammit, I wanted to be *home*, where 13:18 meant 1:18.

I wanted to be *home*, where I could handle a bitchy nurse, and where doctors were called doctors and where my friends could visit me and bring me *People* magazines and pace with worry instead of cramming my tiny room with thousands of flowers, as if I were already dead.

An uneasy feeling washed over me, one that I knew all too well. I didn't mind being *alone*, but this was a kind of alone I'd felt only once before and didn't want to feel ever again. My biggest and most terrifying bout of depression slammed me right after *3rd Rock* hit the airwaves. Which was perfect, because as I think we've already established, I'm obviously quite skilled in the art of *bad timing*. I knew I should be HAPPY, SUPER-DUPER HAPPY. Everyone was THRILLED for me. After all, hadn't I worked my ass off my whole life for this? Wasn't this everything I'd ever dreamed of, surpassing even my wildest fantasies? Yep. And yet I was only filled with anxiety and grief.

Not until years later did I understand why. I no longer had the one thing that safely protected me from having to look too closely at myself: I no longer had ambition.

Most people don't know this, but ambition is one of life's great painkillers. And I had it in *droves*. How could I possibly have any concept of who I really was or what hurt me or what I liked or didn't like when all my thoughts, power, energy, and passion were poured into "succeeding"?

I had always wisely understood that I wasn't exactly an ingenue and was convinced that success, if it came at all, would come much later, when I was old, like in my thirties. Which of course meant that, because of my aforementioned timing issues, I wasn't in any way prepared for the success that slammed me face-first right into the pavement. Overnight, at age twenty-seven, without so much as a warning, I was suddenly far more successful than I *ever* could have imagined. Which should have been lovely, except that in that exact moment, the one thing that drove me for years, my stabilizing force, the one thing that prevented me from having to really feel things or really know myself—my ambition—was ripped away.

I was bereft, in deep mourning, and I couldn't, *for the life of me*, fathom why. I suppose I was also grieving for the loss of the unfeeling, jokey, impenetrable me. I was constantly filled with a sense of dread and overwhelming anxiety, and I was baffled. It felt like I had been kidnapped and shoved into a suffocatingly tiny, dark, airless closet with nothing but myself to keep me company. Like Patty Hearst's, my will was utterly broken by the dark room that was now my mind.

A huge percentage of the recovering drug addicts I know seem to have a few things in common, other than their disease: intelligence, creativity, individualism, humor, and, yes, they all seem to have or have once had enormous amounts of ambition.

Now, don't get me wrong, plenty of drug addicts are just narcissistic, suicidal, boring, or simply mentally ill. I've come across a few in church basements all over this fine city I live in. And obviously there are many reasons one becomes addicted to drugs or alcohol: genetics, a trauma, access, peer pressure, childhood abuse, boredom, depression—the list goes on and on. But I truly believe that one of the main culprits of my addiction was the loss of my burning need to succeed.

Oh, you probably wouldn't have noticed, at first. But ever so slowly, the more successful I got, the more unhappy I was. Then, the harder I tried to fake being "normal" and "happy," the more I failed miserably at it. My emotions were all over the place; one day I'd be fine and perky, the next I'd be grief-stricken and morose. As a happily weeping John Lithgow said to me a few years ago when I told him I was now sober and much happier in my life, "You know, I always knew something was really devastating you and you were battling some demons. But I was always amazed at how you were able to push it aside and do such great work." (*His* words, not mine, okay?)

He followed that with one of the reasons I was doomed to remain sick and suffering for so long: "When it came to doing your job, you'd never know anything was wrong." (See what I mean about "functioning addiction" being the worst kind?)

My loss of ambition quickly morphed into an all-consuming depression, and as anyone can tell you, depression and addiction absolutely adore each other. Just when my depression became too difficult for me to battle alone, I discovered, purely by chance, that narcotics made everything much better, for about four hours. Of course the problem with "treating" depression with drugs or alcohol is that your sorrow then simply becomes one hard ball of *need*. So instead of being depressed, you're simply a sobbing loser who counts pills or constantly vomits on your friends' laps. You've become a poor imitation of someone being alive. But, hey, it's better than being depressed! Isn't it?

Lying in this bed in London, I started to feel those closet walls close in on me again, which filled with me with grim panic.

There doesn't seem to be anyone around. . . .

After a long, sleepless, *click*-filled night, it was morning. Once my vitals were checked by Florence Nightmare-gale—*Why, and a good morning to you, sunshine!*—a dashing young doctor almost as hot as Mr. James swept into my room. Maybe they purposely hire hot doctors as recompense for the curmudgeonly and occasionally nasty nurses? I tried to smile winningly at him, which I instantly regretted because it pulled on my nose tube and made my eyes water in pain. *Ouch.*

He was busy looking at my chart, thank God.

I had now gone four days without showering, which perhaps I could've pulled off back in the old days, back when I had a stomach. I honestly can't imagine how he managed to resist me. But he did.

He cleared his throat and introduced himself as Dr. Smythson-Jones, and I instantaneously knew these three things about him: he was an excellent doctor, he was an arrogant, womanizing prick, and he smoked like a fucking chimney.

Yummy, exactly my type.

Unfortunately, at that same instant I knew that I was most definitely *not* his. I wondered what the reason was, other than the fact that I wasn't a bulimic, twenty-year-old model. Could it be the horrors coming out of my nose tube, the clammy odor of eau de disaster emanating from my every pore, or that I was weeping uncontrollably?

He cleared his throat again. "Ms. Johnston. I'm part of your surgical team, and I must tell you, we're all a bit transfixed by your case. You see, not one of us had ever come across anything as shocking as the condition your intestines were in, at least in someone alive. Truly, it was as if a bomb had gone off. It took us hours to clean up the mess. In fact, we're all rather amazed that you managed to pull through."

Oh, so *that* was it. I guess putrid intestines were a deal-breaker for him. What a shallow asshole.

"When can I eat or drink?" I whined.

"Not for another day or two, when we remove your stomach tube. And then I'm afraid only liquids for three days."

A fresh geyser of tears squirted out.

He cleared his throat once again, which I quickly realized was his way of saying, *You're in England, m'dear. Stiff upper lip, if you please!*

"I must say, I'm rather surprised you're hungry."

"I'm not, really, I just want . . ."

"A cigarette?"

Oh my God, was he hot *and* psychic?! Then I

remembered the party line: cigarette smoking caused an ulcer that then burst.

"Yes, yes, I really just want a cigarette."

"Mm-hmm!" He nodded smugly, as if to say, *That was precisely my diagnosis.* "Well, do keep in mind that one of the reasons you're *so* highly emotional is that you're withdrawing from nicotine, as well as recuperating from a very invasive procedure. Now, I'll confess that I smoke, (*as if I didn't smell it the second you got out of the elevator, Dr. Dickhead*) and must say I'm really quite sympathetic to your plight. I quit once and it was absolutely horrific. I wept for days."

Despite his condescending, model-adoring personality, I found myself kind of liking this guy. I wondered if he'd lend me his blazer to smell, just for a few hours?

"I'll tell you what." He leaned forward conspiratorially. "How would you like a bahth?"

Did he mean *bath*? I pictured him sexily trying to wash my crusty hair.

"I'll call the nurse to help you." *Oh, right. That makes more sense.* "I truly think you'll feel loads bettah after a nice hot bahth."

To make him happy, I said, "You know, that does sound mahvelous."

He left and must have really cracked the whip, because just a scant three hours later my nurse shuffled in. I honestly don't remember her name. I kinda want to call her Vagina Mouth, but for decorum's sake let's go with Nurse Wretched. Now, to be fair, in her defense I can't begin to imagine how difficult a nurse's job must be. The smells, the pooping, the sores, the vomit, the whining, the dying . . . all for next to no money. But back then, I didn't care about any of that. All I knew was that the one person I saw the most often at the very worst time in my life seemed to resent me simply because I'd had *the gall* to be placed on her floor.

She rolled her eyes. "All right now, baf time. Doctuh's odus."

She then brought in some sort of plastic chair, and through the open door to my bathroom I watched her place it in the tub. Then, with great reluctance, she started the arduous journey toward me.

Trust me, babe, I'm not all that excited, either.

Nurse Wretched unplugged me from all the machines— *bye-bye, Mr. M, I'll be right back*—except the nose tube, still connected to the blech-filled pouch. She took the pouch off the hook and unceremoniously plopped it on my legs. What an honor, I had been bequeathed the blech! After about ten long minutes, I was finally untethered. She pushed a button and the bed made a loud bang, which scared whatever crap I had left out of me. Soon I realized the bed was slowly, creakily moving me into a sitting position.

"Swing your legs to the side and stand. But do it slow. Slow, eh? I don' want a big girl like you fallin' on me."

Oh, isn't that smashing. Even in the hospital, I'm given shit about my height. Lord have mercy. Just to be ornery, I quickly started to stand, and regretted it instantly. White-hot agony pierced my gut through the protective curtain of painkillers and I saw white stars.

She sat me back down and scolded me that I had gotten up too quickly. Once the pain had backed down to a dull roar, I croaked, "Sorry, I'm not an expert at the postsurgery stand." I thought I felt her smile as she readied me for try number two. Or it could've been a grimace. Together, we slowly, slowly began the journey from sitting to standing. Well, crouch-standing would be more appropriate.

It was then that I understood her height comment. Even as an upside-down L, I positively *dwarfed* her. Nurse

Wretched was *tiny*. Like, a few inches shy of being a little person. No wonder she was worried. If I fell on her, chances were pretty good she'd be crushed to death. I was sorely tempted, but in the end I decided it would just be too much bother.

But *damn* if she wasn't a strong little thing. She carried most of my almost two hundred pounds (I was busy holding the blech), and we slowly inched our way to the bathroom—*Look, Mommy, Grandma's walking!* Then she carefully helped me get into the tub-chair.

The only problem was that by now I was utterly exhausted. I couldn't even reach the tiny bottle of shampoo next to me, let alone lift my hands to my head.

A spurt of shame reddened my face. "I'm sorry, I need help, I can't wash . . ."

"It's noffing, I do this all the time."

As she washed me (with the exception of my privates. *I'll handle that area, thank ye kindly*) and shampooed my hair three times, I realized that this might be the first time in my adult life I asked someone for help. Then actually let them.

She had definitely done this before and was thankfully quite businesslike. But she was also surprisingly gentle. I can still remember the simple joy I felt at being cared for. And the amazing, unbelievable difference I felt being *clean*. For days I had felt like some revolting, non-human, half-dead creature, like the swamp thing or the elephant man. But as that water rinsed the days of horror away—*I am not an animal, I'm a human being*—I was mesmerized as the gore finally drained away, gone forever. As she towel-dried my hair, I'd never felt so powerfully *alive*. I felt baptized.

While I had been in the bahth, someone had changed the sheets on my bed. *Well, cot, really, but I'm not complaining! It's fine!* Wee Nurse Wretched patiently inched me over, got me in bed, and proceeded to attach me to everything again. *And a* click, click, click *back to you, Mr. M!* I snuggled into the warm (*only slightly scratchy*) sheets, and after every bag was on its correct hook and everything inserted in its proper place, she went to the closet, took out a bunch of blankets, and put them on my legs. Then, in her special tender/brusque manner she actually *tucked me in*, which made me wonder if it had felt as good the last time someone had done this for me, over thirty years ago.

All grown-ups should tuck each other in, it's lovely, I

thought sleepily. For the first time in a very, very long time, maybe years, I felt simply happy.

"Thank you so much, really," I said, smiling at her. Which of course made her roll her eyes and shuffle toward the door. Then she stopped and looked at me as if she wanted to say something.

"Hmmm . . . Yes. Hmmm. G'night, Ms. Johannson." With a nod, she shut off the light and gently closed the door.

"G'night, Nurse Wretched," I said softly into the inky blackness.

I think we're alone now,
There doesn't seem to be anyone around.

Click.

nine

THE SUFFOLK
STRANGLER

in the first week or so postsurgery, the doctors said I'd need at least three weeks of recuperation in the hospital. However, since I played a nurse on *ER* for six episodes, I was quite sure that two would be more than enough. Which is precisely what I told Sonia, the brilliant producer of the play, when she visited me on the fifth day.

Sonia is shrewd, tough, brutally honest, and insanely successful at what she does. Sonia does not, however, have a soothing bedside manner, and she couldn't disguise the dawning horror on her face as her eyes drank in the Freak show laid out in front of her.

When people visit you in the hospital, they bring in fresh air and ruddy cheeks and life. But soon, this remarkable transformation occurs—they seem to become *part of* the hospital. It's an astonishing thing to bear witness to—all the life drains out of them, any amusing story they couldn't wait to share on the way over becomes stuck to the roof of their mouth. The bouquet of peonies in their hand wilts. They enter smelling like Chanel No. 5 or soap, but leave trailing the subtly unpleasant scent of death, Pine-Sol, and formaldehyde in their wake. The hospital sucks everything delightful, new, and fresh out of you. Like the hotel in *The Shining*, it wants you.

Every now and then I was struck by the queasy thought that if that was what happened to someone who was here ten minutes, what in God's name was it doing to me? But I'd furiously *click click click* until that thought was banished.

Since the cast of *Love Song* (bad title, but trust me, excellent play) was only four people, we had all grown very close over the course of the intense four-week rehearsal. They were all so lovely and terribly understanding of my plight. I wonder how kind they would have been if they knew the *real* reason my guts blew up? They each visited a few times and e-mailed and called. Thank God for them. Other than the people involved with the show, my only visitors were my friends Joanna and Daisy. Cillian, the stunning Irish actor who played my brother in the show, seemed traumatized by the place and basically tossed the book he'd brought for me on the bed, kissed the air near my cheek, and backed out. I remember watching him as his walk turned into a run down the endless, Jim Bob Kubrick–designed corridor. How could I blame him? If I could've figured out how Nurse Wretched cranked this bed into sitting, I would've hobbled right on out after him. I'd be drizzling blech, it's true. And I'd be bent in half. But I'd be free.

One of the most endearing qualities about Sonia is her inability to bullshit. Most people seemed to fear her, but I've always had a soft spot for an up-front gal who doesn't seem to need to please others. Sadly, a rare breed. So it didn't surprise me one bit that she was easily able to ignore the life-sucking desires of the hospital. She was too busy dealing with the dawning comprehension that her brand-new smash-hit show on the West End had turned into a rotting money-pit overnight.

It was through her sharp, green eyes that I finally saw what I *really* looked like. And it was really, really bad. I watched those horrified eyes as they slowly traveled from my tremulous smile to the thick tube coming out of my nose, down to my enormous neck catheter, then finally to my bandaged, IV-scarred arms, which is where they stayed for a beat, before finally closing as the full ramifications of my state forced her to fall into a nearby chair.

I can't even fathom being the producer of a huge show, spending loads of money on a West End theater, bearing the enormous cost of flying actors over from America, taking care of their lodging, and issuing paychecks for everyone in production. Not to mention the many thousands of pounds spent on press. All gone, in an instant, simply because you were dumb enough to hire a drug addict. (Although in her defense, she just thought she had hired a smoker who was having a run of very, very bad luck.)

The other thing about being a patient is that all you talk about when people call or visit is *WHAT HAPPENED*. Once that story's told (with slight embellishments each time, just to keep it interesting for yourself), there isn't a whole lot either of you seem capable of discussing.

In Sonia's case, however, she wasn't the least bit interested in what happened. (Which was a shame, really, because this time they were going to bash the door in to get me.) I had barely begun my tale when Sonia looked me dead in the eyes and said, "Kristen. How long?"

Something made me say, "Two weeks, tops."

"Is that what they said? I mean—" She waved toward the piles of accoutrements I was wearing.

"Yes. Sonia, I heal really fast. In fact, I may be back sooner."

I somehow convinced us both, and thus the show went on, with my insanely miscast, twenty-three-year-old understudy taking my place. This brave young girl was the understudy for both myself and the younger Neve Campbell, and to me it was amusingly clear which actress they thought might have had a sick day or two. Because never, in any universe, would this lovely young English lass be cast as the take-charge, demanding, workaholic New Yorker in her forties who has suffered a long, unhappy marriage to Michael McKean. She could have played our au pair perhaps, if the playwright had been generous enough to give us children.

So there I stewed, still as a mummy, as every night my role in the hit play I had worked so hard on was performed by someone else. Someone who wasn't a stupid drug addict. Someone who, miscast as she was, actually *deserved* to be working. I had only two things to keep me warm on those long, mind-numbing days and endless, ice-cold nights: my morphine drip and my tiny nemesis, Nurse Wretched.

Well, that's not completely true. After the first week, I gave in and figured out how to pay for the television, which generously offered three stations. I was happy to discover English soaps are as dumb, if not dumber, than ours. I was begrudgingly becoming invested in pudgy Beatrice's unrequited love for the gorgeous, and clearly gay, Tomás, when, like manna from heaven, all shows were interrupted by the news that some asshole had decided to become a serial killer in the English countryside.

I couldn't believe it.

My friends have always marveled at my endless fascination and thorough knowledge of almost every serial killer who's ever existed. Most find it disturbing, but I know that the seeds were innocently planted by my mother, who adored all murder mysteries.

One day, my father, who was equally devoted to both travel and frugality, bought a houseboat called *Big Toot*, which we would sail up and down the Mississippi River for weeks every summer. *Big Toot* was moored somewhere near St. Louis, I think. So just to *get* to the boat we'd all be living on for *weeks* meant we'd already have spent days together in the car. This became known as "Quality Family Time."

The best part of these road trips (besides their glorious completion) was when my mother could be coaxed into telling us every detail of whichever Agatha Christie or Sherlock Holmes murder mystery she was reading at the time. I'll never forget the spectacular fear and excitement we all felt once she gave in and began to tell the tale of *The Hound of the Baskervilles* for the sixth time as our wood-paneled station wagon raced through the moonless Midwestern night.

Thus, a crime freak was born. Now, I love all books, fiction and nonfiction, with equal measure, but my favorites have always had a macabre leaning. In terms of television, if you saw what I have taped on my DVR, I think there's a good chance you'd back quickly out of my apartment and run for help. Chances are you'd see titles like *Nightmare on Blood Mountain*, *The Dark Side of Daniel*, *Serial Killers: Up Close and Personal*, or *The Mind of Manson*. As well as every episode of *48 Hours*, *Dateline*, and *20/20*.

To be honest, I've never thought much about this

little quirk of mine. I know I have no desire to kill or to ever know a serial killer, and I have zero admiration for them. I suppose that watching these shows brings me back to the excitement I felt every time my mom would say, "Well, it all began on a very dark and foggy night on the moors . . ."

That's why, safely mummified in my London hospital bed, I gratefully lost myself in the search for the Suffolk Strangler. Instead of being creeped out, I felt safe and snug, almost as if I was with my family again, together in our station wagon as it raced toward *Big Toot*.

It didn't matter to me that they'd run the same fuzzy photo of the same victim a hundred times an hour. I was transfixed when they found the bodies of victims number four and five in the woods, even though they'd endlessly replay footage taken from a helicopter so far away that it could've been of a family having a picnic in Arkansas. None of it mattered. I was enthralled. Entranced. I was *Other*.

Even though I'm terribly sorry for those poor prostitutes and their grieving families, that fat, crazy, murderous fuckhead did one good thing in his whole sorry excuse for a life: he unknowingly helped a lonely American pass hundreds of friendless, nicotine-free hours in a London hospital.

Before I knew it, it was time to remove the tube of blech. Thankfully, I have no memory of how that was dealt with. I just know it was gone, which meant I could swallow, which meant I could drink water. Unfortunately, an unfamiliar nurse (I guess *somebody* thought I wouldn't notice if she took a sick day) was allowed to bring me only occasional tiny cardboard shot glasses filled with lukewarm, slightly sulfuric-tasting water. Not exactly the ice-cold bottle of Poland Spring I'd been fantasizing about for the past week.

I'd been bitching to anyone that would listen that I needed food—*cigarettes*—for a week, which I know drove them bonkers. I mean, I know this for a fact, because when I finally read my hospital file years later, this was a common entry: "Patient complained again of pain. Is v. hungry and v. unhappy. Asked to see a Doctor for permission to eat and more morphine.—Nurse W."

Therefore, when I was finally given permission to eat,

I simply couldn't believe that all they'd had to do to shut me up in the first place was to simply put that tray of what they referred to as "breakfast" in front of me. Honestly, it was so disgusting and smelled so vile, my appetite ran as far away as fast as it could and wouldn't be seen again for almost a year.

The food in England has thankfully come a long way from the days when I visited London with my family as a child, when blood pudding was the favored dish in most restaurants. Once, when I was around five, my family had rented a house close to Hyde Park for a few months. Other than a deep, powerful, and thankfully brief crush on Ringo Starr (mostly just to be different. And because I felt sorry for him. And he was a drummer.), the strongest memories I have of London consist of a magical afternoon my mom took us to a movie theater to see a rerelease of *The Sound of Music*, and the fact that I hated all of the food. And I was no picky, American, french-fries-only eater. I loved absolutely all food, ranging from vegetables and fish to fast food (which we were allowed very rarely). My mother was a fantastic cook who actually read *Gourmet* magazine for fun. I was a fan of steak tartare by the time I was a toddler. But in London in the early seventies,

all food, even the candy, which always left one with a sus-
piciously plastic aftertaste, was disappointing.

If this book ever makes its way across the pond, I'd
probably be about as popular there as Jane Fonda would
be at a Vietnam-veterans' convention. However, I'm
counting on the fact that the British seem to have a sense
of humor about themselves that most Americans do not.
They kind of love "taking the piss" out of themselves. I
hope they remember that if they stumble across this book
in the ninety-nine-pence bin. Ironically, I adore London;
next to New York, it's my favorite city. (I'd say Paris, too,
but I've been there twice, once when I was too young
to care, and then as a teen with my mom and step-dad,
when I was deep in the throes of despising everyone and
everything.) But I've spent quite a bit of time in the UK,
and never had a bad time there. Until my guts blew up.

I think that when you get really, really sick, it's as if
you've put on glasses that make you see all things through
vicious and cruel lenses. I'm pretty sure that if my ulcer
had decided to blow up during a yoga retreat at a Bud-
dhist temple, I'd more than likely be writing about what
assholes the monks were. Actually, come to think of it, if
that had happened, I'd probably be dead, and the world

would have been spared yet another "actress addicted to booze and pills tells all!" book.

I was happy to discover that the food in England got better and better each time I went there. Pre-burst, I'd been living a few blocks from King's Road, which had plenty of delicious food shoppes. Wonderful cheeses, meats, soups, fish . . . and of course hundreds of different wines. I'd haul my bloated, fat ass over there after every rehearsal and buy every little thing my rotting tummy desired. I'll never forget my last meal *before*. It was a smoked-salmon roll with cream cheese and a bottle of a crisp, light pinot grigio. If I'd known that it would be almost two months before I would eat anything resembling a meal, I would've *at least* had dessert.

But to describe the food they presented me with as disappointing would be a true understatement. (In fact, calling it "food" wouldn't be accurate either.) Nauseating, unpleasant, and downright gruesome would be in the right ballpark. On the tray was a single plate, and one glance at its contents, two globs of runny yellow and mushy beige, and my appetite was gone in an instant. When I was told the two piles were eggs and porridge, I had to carefully look away and with pleasant urgency beg them to remove it as quickly as possible. Vomiting right now just simply wouldn't do.

It took me a month to want food again. It would be two years before I experienced the sensation of hunger. Even after I was out of the hospital, I couldn't seem to muster up the ability to eat much of anything. It was as if the surgeons had accidentally messed with my taste buds while they were in there, because everything—whether a bowl of chicken broth or a salad—*everything* seemed to carry the unappetizing stench of beef stew with it. (This all led to my eventual label of "ANOREXIC!" Which is funny only because an eating disorder is pretty much the one addiction I've never had.)

After two weeks, I was able to meander up and down the corridor unassisted. I took grim satisfaction the day I managed to outhobble Mr. New Hips in the hallway. *Watch how the youngsters do it, old man!* I was healing nicely.

Too bad they didn't offer a free lobotomy at the same time, because even though my body seemed to be healing rapidly, my brain was still pretty fucked up. Every day someone from the show would call, anxious for my status. It became clear that they were losing bucketloads of money each show I wasn't in. Unfortunately, this wasn't because I'm some huge theatrical draw, but it turns out most people want to see the play with the full cast the director rehearsed. I couldn't take the guilt anymore, so I finally simply took the bull by the horns and (much to the disapproval of my surgeon) announced to everyone that *I WAS LEAVING!*

I convinced the hospital staff that I wouldn't go back to the play for another week of course (lie), and that I could recuperate much faster at home (true). I happened to have a friend who was staying with me (lie), and home was the best place for me so I could eat real food and gain some weight back (offensive but true).

Two days later, just before Christmas, I packed up my meager belongings, signed myself out, made sure I got my painkillers (with three refills. Just in case. Better safe than sorry), and got into a cab just before I almost fainted and ruined my escape plans. Face-planting into the lap of a wheelchair-bound old lady in the lobby might have ruined my triumphant departure.

Finally, freedom. I rolled down the window and let the gloriously crisp winter air rush in. As I rode through the streets of London and giddily watched the Christmas bustle, my mind drifted to wee Nurse Wretched. She was on Christmas break and had sadly missed my dramatic exit. I wondered what her reaction would be when she clocked in for her shift in a few days. Would she sullenly saunter toward my room, practicing her eye roll? She probably wouldn't even notice. And if she did, she probably wouldn't even care.

I couldn't believe that thought actually depressed me. I guess it was because she was the only person alive other than my mother who had both washed my hair *and* tucked me in. She had a bad attitude while doing these, it's true. But like all true lunatics, the meaner someone was to *me*, the more I adored *them* (see: almost every one of my ex-boyfriends).

I had the cab wait as I shopped for food, which ended up being six boxes of Kraft macaroni and cheese, a box of saltines, and a twelve-pack of Coke. London cabbies are way better than New York cabbies. They speak English, and they actually know the city. Plus, they're usually really nice, most likely due to the insanely inflated amount of money they charge. My cabbie that night was especially benevolent. Seeing that I could barely walk, let alone carry anything, he kindly took my bags and my package of American sundries into the Elizabethan elevator and escorted me to my door.

"Thank you, sir, I'm fine now."

"You sure, miss? You look a bit off."

I demurred, tipped him, and shut the door. I was alone. All alone. I barely had a chance to notice how tidy and spotless everything was (*God, they must've hired one hell of a cleaning crew*) before I carefully lay on the bed and fell into a dark, black sleep.

Hours later, I awoke in a panic just as hands were squeezing my throat. Gasping for air, I waited for the sweet relief that comes when you realize, *It's only a nightmare.* However, that relief never came. Because the hands that had been choking me didn't belong to a pudgy, prostitute-hating serial killer. Instead, the hands ruthlessly strangling me had been my very own.

ten

THE GHOST
OF CHRISTMAS
YET TO COME

my reentry to the show was like being met with a less-than-glorious trumpet blast, as if the trumpet player suffered from severe emphysema. All sounds, movements, my entire world now seemed to be encased in a vat of honey. I had never felt more lethargic in my life. Of course I told everyone that the doctors were all just amazed at my recovery, and that they had given me the all clear to perform. Unfortunately, while not physically laborious, the role of Joan was full of angry tirades and she emotionally veered from rage to humor to sorrow. In other words, not quite befitting someone who'd had major intestinal surgery a mere two weeks before.

I also discovered that the painkiller the hospital had

prescribed was tramadol, a much weaker, synthetic form of codeine that won't cause stomach ulcerations. Which was a bit like giving a grizzly bear with a shattered pelvis an aspirin.

Once in my dressing room, I tried to begin my preshow ritual but found it almost impossible. When I wanted to brush my hair, for instance, instead of a quick, thoughtless action, it took a monumental amount of physical and mental effort. *That's my hand reaching for my brush, it's close, I'm almost there, and now I have to put my fingers around its handle and I've got it, no problem, except now I should lift the brush to my hair—ow, that hurts my tummy to reach up, better to just move my head closer to the brush—maybe if I just rest my forehead on the dressing-room table. That's perfect! Now brush. One stroke is fine, I'm too tired.*

The dresser came in to help me get into the newly taken-in version of my costume, and I found I had to sit and catch my breath between each pant leg. Even with drastic tailoring, we soon discovered that I'd need a belt to keep them up. When she ran off to find one, I glanced up and saw my face in the mirror. My face looked as if it had been etched in white marble. I tried to warm up my voice or say one of my lines, but I could barely draw breath to *speak*, let alone *project* to an enormous theater. This was the first moment I had an inkling that maybe, just maybe, the doctors had been right, and I had made a terrible mistake. *No, that's ridiculous! You'll be fine once the adrenaline hits. You absolutely made the right decision.*

Thinking back on it now, I concede that I was one fucked-up bunny. But back then, I had a very different set of beliefs. I believed I could—and *should*—override anyone else's rules and play by my own. Because for many, many years, whatever I *wanted* to happen eventually *did*, simply by the sheer force of my own willpower. (*Well, except for quitting drugs or booze, but that'll happen any day now.*)

Why wouldn't I believe I had control over my destiny? After all, this was proven true to me, time and time again. "You'll never make it," "You're not a real actress, the best you can hope for is sketch comedy," and "Physically, it will be almost impossible for you to get work" were just a few of the constructive pearls of wisdom said to me by various acting teachers. But hadn't I proven them false? I'd been supporting myself as an actress since I was twenty-five years old. And since less than 10 percent of professional actors make more than $5,000 per year, the odds certainly were not in my favor. (That tiny percentage is *way* higher than stage actors who support themselves by doing theater, which I'm going to boldly claim is 00.01 percent. The number would be zero if not for Nathan Lane.)

I beat the odds, regardless of all bets against me, causing me to misguidedly assume that I was in control of my life. Some ridiculously handsome surgeon was no match for my wants and needs. I do what I want, when I want to, and that way everybody's happy. God, I wish I'd known me back then—I sound completely irresistible. I finally understand why droves of my friends dropped everything they were doing and flew over to be with me.

At any rate, it was probably toward the end of the second show that I became aware that I felt just truly awful. But I figured, *Hello! This is what people feel like while recuperating from a major surgery, dumbass.* Besides, I'd timed it perfectly. Because of the Christmas break, I only did two shows (not my best work, I'm sure, but I tried) and then had three days off.

My friend Daisy had generously invited me to spend Christmas with her family in the English countryside, which under normal circumstances I would have been thrilled to do. There's nothing I love more than experiencing another country in someone's home, with their family.

Unfortunately, my few days at Daisy's were far from joyous. I seemed to be getting worse by the hour, not better. It's all a bit hazy, but I remember her family were all funny and warm people and that their house was beautiful, charming, and very lived-in, in that special way only the Brits seem to know how to do right, and we Americans try desperately to emulate. Down the path from the main house was a darling little guest cottage, which I had all to myself. And that is basically where I stayed the entire time. Daisy came in a few times, once to ask if I'd like to join the family, they were all watching *A Christmas Carol*.

I wanted to join them, badly. "Which version?"

"The black-and-white one. The oldest one, I think."

Damn! I love that one. I couldn't believe that I was in a gorgeous home in the Cotswolds over Christmas and I couldn't even muster up the energy to *lie* on a couch and watch a film. Instead, as I'd done since my youth, I escaped by immersing myself in a book.

That worked for the first day, until even reading became impossible because the words began to blur together ominously. I also couldn't eat. Meaning literally, for two days, I couldn't put even *one* bite of food in my mouth. It was awful—I was the ghostly guest from hell.

After a long nap I'd convince myself I felt better, that I was over the hump, that I was starting to feel like "me" again. I'd shower, dress, put on some makeup (*Is it the lighting or is my skin lime green?*) and I'd appear, much to almost everyone's relief and cheer. The exception being the children, who had the good sense to stay as far away as they possibly could from this creepy, silent ghoul. One of them, the two-year-old girl, would sob inconsolably from the moment I appeared until a few minutes later when I would quietly disappear again. Walking gingerly down the foggy, moonlit path, tears streaming down my hot, lime-green face, I knew why the children were so terrified. My creepy pallor and hollow eyes combined with my silent presence and long black parka made me a dead ringer for the Ghost of Christmas Yet to Come.

Poor Daisy's mum would sometimes bring me broth, but even that I couldn't manage. This was way more than a lack of appetite. It was as if someone had simply gone into my brain and plucked out the part that allows even a morsel of food to pass one's lips. I couldn't even force myself to eat or drink a thing. Normally I'd think this was kinda cool, especially because of my recent discovery that I was a fat, fat fatty-kins, but all I felt was a hollow dread. Finally I decided to put this wonderful family out of their misery, and the morning after Christmas I called a taxi to take me back to London.

We had a matinee the next day, and when I woke up, I was feverish and extra-lethargic. I tried to take a shower and couldn't stand up without feeling faint. Sobbing and dripping shampoo, I lay on the bed quivering from cold, fear, and frustration as it became clear that I had to call Malcolm to tell him I'd have to miss *yet another* show.

"Get back to 'ospital, right now," he demanded.

I started crying harder. "No! I don't want to go back there! Can't I just go to a private physician and see what he says first?"

"Kristen, you get your bum in a taxi and go to 'ospital immediately, or I'll come over and drag you there myself."

I got my bum in a taxi immediately. I can't put into words the sense of terror and failure I felt as I slowly hobbled into that emergency room again. But as stubborn as I was (am) even I had to concede that I had lost all control of this situation. I also knew that whatever death felt like, this was it. I could feel certain parts inside of me shutting down, and I knew I didn't have long. I was put once again in a curtained-off bed in the ER, except this time I wasn't weeping or screaming. I made no noise at all. I just stared at the ceiling, hating my life and my awful, traitorous body.

I wanted death. I welcomed it. I really did. I couldn't bear going through this again alone. An ER nurse finally showed up, and this time instead of grilling me for information, she took one look at my face (*What, like you've never seen a dying lime-green person before?*), and within seconds I was being wheeled back into the X-ray room. Except seeing it through death goggles instead of agony goggles, I realized what I thought was an X-ray room was actually a fancy-looking CT and MRI area. This time the head technician was incredibly sweet and gently explained that he needed to do a CT scan of my surgical site, to make sure there was no infection.

I could've told him what it took a half hour of frowning and looking at a screen to ascertain: I had an infection and it was a *doozy*. Still, I wasn't prepared when, without warning, he cut a hole just below my left rib cage and shoved a tube into me, which immediately began draining—I'm not sure how much, but it looked to me like four or five of those huge Evian bottles—this yellowy-green liquid. The nurses kept taking the full ones away, and a new one would fill up immediately. This all happened in about ten minutes as I lay there, in shock. I mean, shouldn't I be put under for something like this?

The Evian procedure eventually ended. But the tube remained in me, now draining into a pouch. *Aw, fuck me. Another pouch.* Now, I may not be the sharpest knife in the drawer, but by now even I was savvy enough to comprehend that *a tube connected to a pouch* meant I wasn't going anywhere.

I did feel a bit less dead, however. So as they once again wheeled my bed through the eternal white hallways of my new home, I took out my cell and called the director of the play, John Crowley. The nurse at my feet was about to say "no cell phones" until she saw the look on my face and wisely thought better of it. She turned away just as he answered.

"John, I'm so sorry." I burst into tears as he murmured his sympathies in his comforting Irish lilt. I thought to myself, *Get it together, you fucking pussy. Be professional for once in your life.*

When I finally managed to sound like I wasn't crying,

I said, "Look, John, the bottom line is, I don't know how long I'll be here. It's a really, really bad infection, it could be weeks."

"Don't you worry, we'll make do—"

"No, listen, John. Really listen, okay? You *have* to fire me and hire someone else. This isn't fair to anyone, and I can't handle the stress of you guys waiting for me *again*—"

That's when *he* interrupted *me*. "I'm not firing you, Kristen. I don't care how long it takes. You're who I want in this role. Just take your time, get better, and we'll see you very soon, all right?"

I didn't know what to say. I was truly thrown by his loyalty and knew I hadn't earned it. "I, John . . . I'm just so, so sorry about this."

"Nonsense! Just some bad luck, is all."

I hung up on him before I began to make crying noises.

As it turns out, he was absolutely right. I *was* shit out of luck, because at that very moment, I looked up and saw that I was being wheeled directly toward enormous doors marked ST. SOMEONE'S PUBLIC WARD.

"No, no, no. Stop, please. *Stop!*"

I was finally brought to a halt.

guts

"Yes, miss, what is it?" asked the nurse at my feet.

"There must be some mistake. I'm supposed to be in a *private room.*"

"Yes, well, there are no private rooms available, miss. But you never know, one might open up by the end of the week!" Then she winked cheerfully. I hated her.

We entered the crowded ward. Without Mr. Morphine, this was a completely different place. It was loud, crowded, and stank of death. And through all of that was the unmistakable stench of loneliness. An old man was crying out for his son, who would never come. A weeping woman was bent over a still young girl, while her father was fruitlessly begging for her to wake up. *"Astrid! Oh, Astrid—"* But I knew Astrid would never open her eyes again. Two beds over, Astrid's teenage boyfriend (the driver) was hoarsely weeping, "It wu'nt me fawt, it wu'nt me fawt" over and over and over.

Hell. I had entered hell. I'd always known I'd end up here, I just didn't know I'd have to be alive at the same time. I turned my head toward the wall and longed for someone, anyone, to comfort me. My life wasn't supposed to be like this. I would have given everything I had to be anywhere but this place, so far from anyone and anything I love.

In the middle of the night, a young nurse tapped me gently. "Miss?" she whispered. "So sorry to wake you, but I've got to change your pouch and I didn't want to give you a fright."

"Thanks," I whispered back. After a few moments of silence, I asked, "What's your name?"

No answer. I looked down below the side of my bed and saw that she had disconnected the full pouch and had gone into a spasm of some sort. That's when I realized she was dry-heaving. Three, four times. She even made these little *ayup* noises. I prepared myself for the spray of vomit. But it never came, and a second later she looked up at me, her eyes watering.

"So sorry, miss."

"No, seriously, *I'm* sorry. I guess that stuff smells pretty bad, huh?" I asked as she attached a new, fresh pouch.

She smiled, then put her arm on mine and said warmly, "I'll be quite honest wit'cha. That—" She pointed toward the nasty pouch now safely ensconced in some

closed plastic bin. "Smells far, far worse than anything
I've ever smelled in me life. And I'm *including* rotting dead
people!" She slapped my arm as if to say, *Naughty girl!*

"Oh, all right. Thanks?"

"You'd be quite welcome. Now, get some sleep, you!"
she scolded, as if instead of waking me up, she had caught
me doing jumping jacks or guzzling a beer. She chuckled
and, shaking her head, picked up the offending bin and
hustled away.

You can't really sleep on a hospital ward. Someone's always moaning, crying, begging, pissing, or talking in
that "nurse whisper," which is so loud I'm fairly certain
they could easily be heard in the cafeteria, four floors
down. There is a modicum of privacy, in the form of a
white shower curtain. But the curtains are whisked open
and shut with such shocking speed that you begin to live
in fear of the jarring *shliiiisk* noise. It begins when your
finely tuned ears pick up on the rubbery *boing* sound
of rubber-soled shoes, and suddenly there's a *shliiiisk*
four beds down. You know it's that ancient man with

Parkinson's because he always lets out a terrified yelp. *Phew*, you think, certain you're safe, when *SHLIIISK!!!* and you almost crap your pants.

I'm not sure how long I spent in the ward but it felt like a lifetime. I was given crappy tramadol, and no matter what I said, they wouldn't give me real painkillers. Apparently, a tube jammed into one's ribs doesn't constitute "pain." Which it really doesn't, I suppose. But I wanted to scream, *What about the pain in my head? Or in my heart?* But I knew no one would listen; that kind of pain was handled in a very different kind of hospital. The kind that usually involved the word "institution."

On the third morning, my sexy surgeon Mr. James finally took time off from saving drug addicts' lives and performing gastric bypasses to visit me. He was, as always, surrounded by his worshipful posse of young-uns, which included the dashing nicotine and model aficionado, Dr. Smythson-Jones.

Because I needed to come off as sane and healthy as possible to earn a rapid release, I burst into tears. They were all used to this by now, and collectively sighed, rolled their eyes, or in Dr. Smythson-Jones's case, loudly cleared his throat.

Mr. James, however, just looked at me calmly. I loudly blew my nose into a sandpaper sheet a young girl handed me and then nodded at him to say whatever he came to say.

"Ms. Johnston, you unfortunately have a very serious infection, and although it's rather common with the sort of surgery—"

I interrupted him. "Listen, Mr. James, I appreciate all you've done for me." I tried to sound together and healthy despite the fact that I was noisily weeping. "But you *have* to understand. *I can't stay here.*"

I'll never forget the look on his face: It was true, real anger. I was so shocked I forgot to keep crying.

"Ms. Johnston. Let me be very clear with you." I nodded, chastised. "If you leave this hospital, you will, *without question*, die. I'm absolutely serious."

My face reddened. I'd offended my sexy surgeon. Who does that? I'm an awful person. "Okay."

He looked relieved and put his expressionless Danielle Steel face back on. "Good."

I was flooded with relief. "But, sorry, Mr. James? Really, how long will I be here?"

"Until your infection is gone. I don't really know." He saw the look on my face and added, "I'm terribly sorry, I know it's not ideal. But you have no other options, really."

"I understand." I wanted them gone. I couldn't stand having these healthy young creatures staring down at my ruined body any longer. So I turned my face to the wall, closed my eyes, and longed desperately to be *other*.

Think of something happy, and they'll go away.

A mishmash of memories bombarded me. Of being cradled on my mother's lap in a rocking chair when I was three; my sister and I playing endlessly in our attic playroom; the joy of staying at my beloved Aunt Kay and Uncle Robert's house in Oak Park every summer to take her art classes; feeling so grown-up when I took the train to Chicago by myself at seventeen to audition for NYU; the first boy I kissed outside of a spin-the-bottle game; the day I jumped off the highest rock in a quarry in Vermont; falling head over heels in love for the first time; playing with Beau and Mercy in Connecticut; laughing my ass off with Hickey and Joe on the front lawn of Joe's house in

guts

Sag Harbor; kissing Jimmy Smits at the end of *Much Ado About Nothing* in Central Park under a full moon.

And finally, there was peace, for a moment.

Until the obese woman in the bed next to me moaned, shat, and then died.

Just a li'l reminder that life isn't perfect.

eleven

PAPILLON

"I accuse you of a wasted life!"—Judge

"Guilty. Guilty. Guilty."—Papillon

—FROM THE 1973 FILM *PAPILLON*

i'm convinced that the only people worth knowing are those who've had at least one dark night of the soul. Now, a dark night of the soul is completely different from simply having a very bad night. A very bad night might include being stood up, discovering a rather large canker sore on your lip the eve of your wedding, or when someone excitedly asks you when the baby is due when you haven't had sex in a year.

A dark night of the soul is very, very different. Recovering addicts and alcoholics sometimes refer to this as their "bottom," but it happens to almost everyone, at some point or another. It's that life-changing moment when everything you've always wanted to become, everything you actually are, and everything you know you'll never be, all slam into each other with the deadly force of three high-speed trains. It's the night of your reckoning, the terrifying moment when your mask falls away and you're forced to see what's actually been festering underneath it all these years. You finally see who you *really are*, instead of who you've always *pretended* to be.

My dark night of the soul occurred in a peach-colored hospital room on New Year's Eve, just as 2006 turned into 2007. I had finally been moved back to the private wing, and when Nurse Wretched saw that I was back in her care, she cleverly pretended we had never met before, which made me love her even more. Because there was a skeleton crew due to the holidays, there was only one nurse on duty. And really, who else but she would be my costar on such an important night?

It seemed that almost all of the private rooms had suddenly emptied. "Goddamnit, Carol, I'm telling you, this damn hernia won't keep me from partying on New Year's Eve. Now stop crying, shut up, and wheel me out!" Since New Year's Eve is, without question, my least favorite holiday, I've always been baffled by those who seem to enjoy it. Even when I was a huge lush, New Year's Eve always seemed like the perfect night to curl up with a good book, a bottle or three of wine, and elegantly pass out by 11:00 p.m.

The only patient besides me in the private wing was a silent, dying woman in the room next door. Every day her daughter kept a faithful bedside vigil. I would see her as she passed my room to get tea or speak to one of the nurses in a hushed, worried tone. The daughter appeared to be in her sixties, so in my imagination, her mother was at least a hundred and five. That afternoon, the quiet was suddenly shattered by terrible screams. *"Mum, oh, no, Mum! Please, no, Mum!"* echoed through the halls, and I assumed the old gal had finally given up. During the ensuing hubhub, as the daughter continued to emit the most heartbroken, awful noises, I remembered the nightmarish day I'd been admitted to this place and wondered if perhaps some stupid nurse would tell *her* to shut up, so as not to disturb *me*?

After a long while, all was quiet again as I watched the late-afternoon winter sun slowly fade to dark. From my window I had a stunning view of London, in all its haunting, majestic glory. With the exception of that sunny day, the city was usually shrouded in fog, which matched my mood perfectly. In my new hospital room, the cityscape included a fairly close view of the London Eye, a huge Ferris wheel perched right on the edge of the Thames.

Many months before, the morning after I had arrived from New York, I woke up at three a.m. wide awake and suffering from a bad case of jet lag. I was staying at a hotel until my flat was sorted out. I knew sleep was hopeless, so I decided to go for a walk and ended up aimlessly wandering for hours along the Thames. The sun was just beginning to come up when I spotted the Eye, and I promptly decided that riding it would be the perfect (if a bit touristy) thing to do on my first morning there. What better way to see my new city? Besides, I'd be first in line to ride it; after all, how crowded could it be at a quarter past six a.m.? I quickly got my answer when I spotted the line of hundreds of camera-wielding, pamphlet-shaking tourists impatiently waiting for it to open. I hightailed my overtired ass back to the hotel as fast as I could.

Months later, as a different person, I would endlessly stare at that wheel from my bed as it went around and around and around. It's almost as if I thought that if I stared long enough, somehow I could become one of those lucky people on it, whose only concern was if she should go to Buckingham Palace or Harrods when she disembarked.

As night began to fall, Nurse Wretched came in to check my p.m. vitals.

"They make you work tonight?"

"Hmm." She wrote something down.

"That sucks. I bet your boyfriend's bummed about *that*, huh?" For weeks I'd been pumping her for some tiny morsel, *anything* to help me flesh out what I imagined her world to be. Unfortunately, this was one tight-lipped lady, so my imagination was pretty much doing it all. (Here's where I was so far: A tiny, dingy flat kept ruthlessly tidy. Framed pictures of President Kennedy, Lady Di, and Queen Elizabeth on the wall. A sickly, demanding mum in the back room. Many, many, many cats.)

"You 'ave bow'l movemen' t'day?" she asked.

Or, we could always just talk about that.

"No." *How could I when I eat the equivalent of a saltine a day? At this rate, a poop might happen in July.*

"Cheers." And she was gone.

And that was the full extent of my human contact that entire day.

A few long hours later, I was beginning to doze off when I noticed that a movie I loved when I was younger, *Papillon*, was beginning. That's the thing about English telly, they actually play *old* movies on their major networks. *Papillon* was made in the seventies and stars in the title role one of the most heart-stopping, gorgeous movie stars *ever*, Steve McQueen. Costarring with him was Dustin Hoffman, an actor I usually really like. Unfortunately in *Papillon* he went a bit overboard in the "nutty accent, funny teeth, and kooky eyeglasses" department. Now, I'm the last gal to judge a scenery-chewer, but it's almost as if he said to himself, *Maybe if I whip out every single acting trick in the book, nobody'll notice how much hotter McQueen is.* (Sorry, sweetie, not happening.)

Papillon is based on a book written by this French petty thief of the same name. The events he describes have since been called into question, but it's a damn good movie regardless. For doing almost nothing, Papillon is sent to hell on earth, Devil's Island, which at one time was a real French penal colony in French Guiana, South America. This place was so awful it makes anyone who kvetched about Alcatraz seem like a pussy. I was amazed to find myself smiling, because for the first time in almost two months, I finally saw someone whose life sucked way more than mine.

Papillon soon becomes obsessed with escaping and you really can't blame the guy, what with the heat, the workload, them pesky 'skeeters, the occasional bout of leprosy, and guards who relish torturing for the slightest infraction. With every failed escape attempt he endures more torment and more time is added on to his sentence. Finally, they've had enough of this naughty Frenchman and sentence him to solitary confinement. He spends so many years in complete darkness without proper food or any physical or mental stimulation that by the time he gets out, his hair is white, he can barely walk, and his teeth have fallen out. (Guess who's *still* a fox?)

Finally, he and Dustin are sent to Pig's Island, where they live in little huts and have pigs as pets. They're left there without guards because the cliffs are so high that escape is deemed impossible. Pig's Island always seemed pretty nice to me, if they'd just put up some curtains, give the huts a good cleaning, and maybe pick some wildflowers.

But Papillon doesn't have time for a broom. He refuses to give up the dream of escaping. *He will not be confined.* Besides, Dustin's scenery-chomping would try anyone's patience. Eventually, he somehow figures out by tossing a bunch of coconuts over the cliffs into the ocean that there's one short lull in the tide, and that instead of smashing back against the rocks, one lucky coconut gently floats out to sea. So, he makes a coconut boat, figures out the timing, and floats to freedom and a life as a celebrated writer. Leaving Dustin behind to ponder why the hell he worked so damned hard if McQueen was gonna effortlessly steal the whole movie anyway.

I was at the coconut-throwing scene when I heard a loud bang. Because I'm from New York City, I almost ignored it, assuming it was just someone being murdered. Then, out of the corner of my eye, a burst of orange. I looked up from my bed out the window, and I saw the most glorious, enormous splashes of color lighting up the skyline. Fireworks! I could even hear the "oohs" and the "aahs" floating up from the celebrating crowd.

To this day I don't know exactly why, but for some

mysterious reason, this was the moment that sanity finally chose to break through the madness that had held me in its iron grip for so many years. With no warning, I was struck by this thought:

There are people in that crowd who are looking at the same fireworks I am right this very second who are STONE COLD SOBER. There are people in that crowd who don't feel the need to touch the back pocket of their jeans constantly to make sure the six pills are still there. There are people in that crowd who are simply enjoying the spectacle, without wondering if they have one refill left at the pharmacy, or if they would have to call yet another doctor. There are people out there RIGHT NOW who are with their loved ones and are just happy to be alive.

Grief overwhelmed me. True, real sorrow not for me, but for finally seeing the truth of what I was. A selfish, self-serving, loathsome creature who did nothing to better the world. I finally truly *felt* the weight of all the pain I had caused, all the tears that had been wasted on me, all the gifts I had been given to me that I had just carelessly frittered away, and all of the thousands of hours I had spent obsessing about something as ridiculous, boring, and stupid as *me*.

I don't want this life anymore, I thought. *I can't bear who I've become.*

I squeezed my eyes shut and started praying. I mean really praying, for the first time since I was a little kid. I'm not sure to whom, it wasn't to some guy on a throne, or his son. I didn't believe in those guys anymore. But I prayed to someone or something out there in the universe wiser than I. I prayed to all the people I'd ever loved, and all the people stupid enough to love me back. I prayed to my dead dog Pablo. I prayed to the gorgeous fireworks outside my window, and all the people enjoying them.

I prayed that somehow, someway, a miracle would happen and I'd figure out how to do the impossible— build a raft out of coconuts and escape from my own Devil's Island.

Thirty-nine years old.

Totally alone.

A wasted life.

Happy New Year!

twelve

PRETTY UGLY

new year's Eve was my *bottom*, but it wasn't *the end*. That would happen a few weeks later, due to the fact that I'm a stubborn control Freak. Well that, and the fact that I was fucking crazy.

One fine morning in mid-January my surgical team delivered some amazing news. My infection had almost completely disappeared, and I could finally officially leave! I couldn't believe it. *The nightmare is over. I can't believe it.* But then they informed me that I would be wearing a colostomy bag for the next month to help drain the remaining infection. My smile faltered. Then faded. *A colostomy bag? Aren't those for old people who've had to have their butts removed?* Whenever I pictured a colostomy bag (which, I can assure you, wasn't very often), I had always assumed it to be an enormous blue bag attached to someone's very old, very unhappy rectum.

Oddly, I was wrong. It's actually way more fun. I was going to describe one to you, but I think Wikipedia's definition is way cuter than anything I could rustle up. A quick heads-up first for all you idiots who don't enjoy reading medical journals in your spare time: a *colostomy bag* is actually called an "ostomy pouching system," which I think gives it a much more elegant ring. Oh, and a *stoma* refers to an opening on the body (which in my case was located just below my left rib cage) and is *not* fancy medical lingo for "stomach," which would have been my guess. So sit back, grab a snack, and enjoy!

> An ostomy pouching system (also colloquially called a
> bag) is a medical prosthetic that provides a means for the
> collection of waste from a surgically diverted biological
> system. An ostomy pouching system collects waste from
> the stoma and allows the stoma to drain into a sealed
> collection pouch, while protecting the surrounding skin
> from contamination. Ostomy pouching systems are air-
> and water-tight and allow the wearer to lead an active

*normal lifestyle that can include all forms of sports,
recreation, and even performing in a play.*

I added the very end. Just making sure you're still
with me.

The bag basically looks like a quart-size sandwich bag
with a circular, sticky ring so as to surround your stoma.
One of the twelve-year-old doctors showed me how to
tape it on myself, and I must say, nothing puts a spring
in a girl's step like sporting a darling, pus-filled "ostomy
pouching system."

After spending a total of almost two months in that hospital, I had lost a whopping sixty-five pounds. When I
looked in the mirror above the sink, I was so gaunt and
ghostly white, I looked like I had been on *Survivor: Green-
land*. As I made arrangements to leave, they asked me to
pay the bill. I'd been dreading this part for weeks, and I
almost had a heart attack when I saw it. *I couldn't fucking believe it*: everything—the 7-hour surgery, X-rays, CT
scans, the truckloads of morphine, antibiotics, and many

other medications, the staff, the blech-filled pouch, the private room—*everything*, all of it ended up costing me a whopping two thousand pounds.

Which meant that, in 2007, I owed them a little over three grand.

You have to understand that for *weeks* I had been preparing to give the go-ahead to my business manager to clean out my bank account and pension, sell my apartment, all while agonizing over which treasured family heirloom to sell. I honestly thought it would cost me at least a million bucks. I had been aware that I was in a country that was renowned for its incredible National Health Service (known as NHS). The UK's NHS ensures that *anyone* and *everyone* gets free medical treatment, regardless of *who you are* or *what you do*. I just never imagined it would apply to *me*, an American, pill-popping lush.

Recently, I decided to see what information I could find on the Internet about it, and I almost fell off my chair when I read that one of the few areas of medicine the NHS doesn't cover is dental work. Which explains a great deal. (Personally, I would gently encourage them to revisit that decision.) This means that the *only* thing I was charged for was my private room. Jesus, no wonder Nurse Wretched had a bug up her ass. She washed my hair and tucked me in, and I paid her not one dime.

Discussing America's health-care reform isn't one of my favorite pastimes; however, I must say that I think our system sucks because, soon, the only people who're gonna be able to afford to *go* to doctors will be the fucking *doctors*. Infuriating. I can't imagine what would've happened to me if my guts had decided to blow up in New York City. Well, that's not exactly true. I *can* imagine. You might very likely find me in the San Fernando Valley shooting porn for gentlemen who like their ladies tall, blond, and a bit long in the tooth.

After I giddily paid the bill, I knew I had one last important thing to do before I left. I knew I had to say good-bye to one *very* special person. With a heavy heart, I wandered around the wing and finally found her being rude to someone's devastated family member at the front desk. I grinned and leaned against the wall to watch her for a few minutes, soaking in my last precious moments with her. When she had the balls to simply ignore the hysterically sobbing woman's question, I felt all warm and fuzzy inside. *What a lady.*

I walked up to them, my pouching system sloshing noisily. "Excuse me."

Nurse Wretched turned around quickly and glared daggers at my vagina, which was at her eye level. I watched as her tiny eyes slowly traveled upward until they met mine. She squinted up at me warily.

"Wot."

"Listen, I'm leaving today."

Silence.

"And I just wanted to thank you, so much. For putting up with me, and especially that time you washed my hair and tucked me in. Other than my mom, nobody's ever done that for me before and I—thank you. Really. It meant a lot. I'll never forget you."

She kept staring at me. Then, for the first time since we met almost two months before, Nurse Wretched smiled at me. I was floored. To be honest, I didn't think her face could even *do* that. It didn't matter that she was lacking a front tooth and quite a few bottoms, I thought it was one of the prettiest smiles I'd ever seen.

Then, just as fast as it appeared, it was gone so completely I wondered if I had imagined it. She abruptly turned and walked away, the weeper hot on her heels, begging for answers I knew she would never get.

I finished out the last few months of the play. I was terrifyingly skinny, very weak, and I almost fainted a few times on stage, but I finished it. I wore an "ostomy pouching system" underneath my wardrobe for most of it, but I finished it. I managed to visit a few different doctors under the guise of "I've just had this awful operation, I'm in agony," which worked like a charm and kept me cushioned in a sea of Vicodin. And I still didn't stop to think about what I was doing. Denial. My Kryptonite.

Then, about three weeks before my return to New York, I got Laura's e-mail.

My face still burns with shame when I think of it. Laura is one of my oldest, closest friends. She's a brilliant costume designer, and her two young kids are the kind you actually *want* to spend as much time with as possible. (In my opinion, if you ever want to know what kind of a person someone is, just look at their kids. Or their pets.)

A wee bit of backstory. Many years ago, in the fall of 2001, I was performing in *The Women* on Broadway. At the same time, Laura, who had just given birth to her second child, had to have a bowel resection, which was a surgery similar to mine. She even had the tube of blech coming out of her nose. And yet of course, it was completely different. Hers was a horrible twist of fate, while mine was most definitely not.

I visited her in her private hospital suite at St. Luke's on the Upper West Side almost every day before the show, and between shows on matinee days. I helped her to the bathroom, with the baby, and with whatever else she needed. Therefore, when almost the same thing happened to me (well, at least as far as *she* knew), I was stunned and very, very hurt that she had only called me *one* time, right after I got out of surgery. For two months I would e-mail her and leave her messages, and I'd never hear back. I couldn't believe she could be so cruel. My hurt stewed and twisted and curdled as I lay there with nothing else to do. Every time I'd think of her, it would sting and I'd weep from the betrayal.

Finally, a few weeks after I was out of the hospital, I wrote her an angry, hurt, weepy e-mail. I was not at all prepared for the response. I know it was much longer, with lots of other stuff, but these are the sentences that are burned into my memory:

Kristen, I think you're a drug addict and an alcoholic.
I think you lie to everyone, all the time. We all know
what's been going on with you. And I think your guts
blew up because of how many drugs you take. I love you,
Laura

I sat on the edge of my bed, in my tiny flat on Cadogan Square, trembling, and felt myself disappear into a black hole of nothingness. My mask, ripped away. Laura tore it away. She's a terrible person who hates me. How could she be so mean to me? *Oh my God.*

A second wave of paranoia and panic slammed into me. My friends know? Who? Have they been idly trashing me behind my back?

Nonononononooooo.

White-faced, I just sat there and stared at my feet for hours. How on earth could I possibly tell all my friends, my mom, my sister, my brother? All the people I lied to, all the people who felt just awful that this terrible fate had befallen me? If I told them I didn't exist, that the person they knew and loved was just a mirage, then would I just become . . . nothing?

If I don't exist, who am I?

"No, no, no. Ignore it, it will all go away. Just keep pretending," *He* said sternly.

Oh, thank God, Mr. M, where have you been?

"Right where I've always been. Right where I'll always be."

I took five Vicodin, and I immediately felt much better. Mr. M helped me come up with a brilliant plan. *I'll just stop drinking or taking drugs, and when I get back, I'll just ice them all out. Won't they all feel fucking stupid when they see how wrong they were.*

An English friend came to see the show that night. Afterward, we went to the Ivy, and despite my resolution of just a few hours before, I had three martinis, because that is what I've always done with a friend after a play. Always. I drank because I couldn't fathom *not drinking*. My body wept in protest, my spirit crushed. But I drank anyway.

The next day I woke up, and I knew.

I WILL NEVER, EVER STOP. EVER. I WON'T "GROW OUT OF IT," AND IT WON'T STOP ON ITS OWN. I WILL

guts

DRINK AND USE DRUGS UNTIL I DIE. WHICH WILL BE VERY SOON.

Terrifying.

I needed to talk to someone. I called my friend Marci in New York.

"Marci, I'm worried about my drinking." *Ooh! Maybe I can just be an alcoholic?*

"Well, why don't you just go to rehab and get it dealt with?"

She said this in the same tone one would say, "You should put sunscreen on" or "Have you thought about putting that lamp over there?" Her simple, nondramatic answer piled on top of Laura's bravery saved my life. Laura exposed the rot, and Marci made it sound like something solvable instead of impossible. They both, in their own ways, cajoled my illness from the deep cavern of shame and self-hatred it had been rotting in and brought it out into the open.

Yeah, why don't I? People do it every day. Besides, my way isn't exactly working out so good anymore. Suddenly, I could almost picture myself clean and better and whole. Maybe I don't have to live as if I'm already dead. Maybe I can live as if I'm alive. I could hear Mr. M shouting angrily, but his voice got weaker and weaker. I immediately called a few places and finally reached the Meadows, a facility in Arizona. Before I could talk myself out of it (or Mr. M got wind of it), I booked a bed for the week after I got home from London.

And that, *finally*, was the beginning of the end.

A confluence of four events that had built into a perfect storm. The hospital, the *Papillon* fireworks, the e-mail from Laura, and the phone call with Marci. If just one of those things hadn't occurred, I'm certain I'd still be using (on the off chance I was still alive, that is). But the fact that each had transpired, one after another, in the order they did, is what saved me.

My last days in London were consumed by a coconut-size ball of fear that had formed in the pit of my ravaged guts. But instead of trying to kill it, I took that goddamn coconut and used it to begin to build my raft. A sorry, poorly made, leaky fucker that still somehow managed to sail me all the way to rehab.

I'm not going to go into minute detail about my experience in rehab, because really, haven't we read enough books about that? However, if you are brave enough to go, I have just a few pieces of advice: *Shut the fuck up and listen for once in your life.* And even if your counselor has a dream catcher above her desk, I don't care, listen anyway. Oh, and people who are your best friends in rehab will very likely ring your doorbell two months later with tiny coke rocks falling out of their noses, asking if they can crash on your pullout.

So go there to get better. Not to be adored by everyone. That one took me a while.

Last, if you're scared to go, imagine walking into the cafeteria for your first shaky meal only to be greeted by the sounds of trays dropping and people freaking out as they recognize you (hey, rehab's a fairly monotonous place). Imagine being treated to a lengthy, daily sermon from some bizarre alcoholic writer who claimed to be a fan (?) of *3rd Rock* and who felt he could improve upon story lines you now no longer even remember. Or imagine coming out of the shower on your first morning there only to be greeted by the vision of your roommate rifling through your luggage. Okay? So man up, get over yourself, and think, *If so-and-so could do this, so can I.* (My reference was Kate Moss.)

One life-changing thing happened to me while I was there. My counselor, Grace, was one tough-as-nails lady. She wasn't charmed by me at all; in fact, she reminded me of a tiny British nurse I once knew. Someone who had taught me well the delicate art of navigating those who are both diminutive and rude. Therefore, around my second week there, I pulled Grace aside in the cafeteria and boldly said, "I think I'm trying to get you to like me."

"Gee, ya think?" she said.

I was taken aback. "Is it *that* obvious?"

She then rolled her eyes (I swear) and said, "Kristen, why don't you stop worrying about how everyone else feels about you and start concentrating on yourself? How do *you* feel about people? How do *you* feel about situations? Because right now all I see is someone who doesn't have a clue as to who she really is or what she really wants."

My face went hot. I was about to tell her she had her head up her ass, but I couldn't. I knew she was right. Then she softened a bit and said, "Kristen, isn't it time you learned how to see yourself through your *own* eyes, instead of everyone else's?"

guts

I looked at her, lost. Fragile. Empty. Speechless. For some reason, this made her happy. She grinned and said, "Well, *there* you are, Kristen. Welcome to rehab."

I left Arizona dazed and confused, with nothing to show for my thirty days but my sobriety, a coin they give you to remember to *stay* sober (helpful!), and a bunch of shitty turquoise jewelry from the rehab store. Here's another thing about rehab—if you're a stimulation junkie (and what addict isn't?) the utter drudgery of spending day after day learning about your disease and discussing your addictions ad nauseum in group therapy, with a few private therapy sessions thrown in, not to mention endless chats with fellow patients trying to see who has the most embarrassing wedding story or funniest DUI moment, the bottom line is—even though rehab is good for you, it's profoundly fucking boring. Thus, I became obsessed with purchasing anything I could get my hands on in the rehab store. These treasures included *IT WORKS IF YOU WORK IT SO WORK IT YOU'RE WORTH IT* key chains, kitchen magnets with sayings like "Don't run so fast that your guardian angel can't keep up!" and a couple hundred dollars' worth of turquoise nonsense.

Maybe this'll help you understand the depth of the boredom: Upon my mother's arrival for "family week" (God bless her), she had in her purse some Juicy Fruit gum and a rolled-up copy of *More* magazine. *Contraband!* I grabbed them from her purse as fast as I could and threw them under my bed.

"Why did you just—"

"Nevermind, Ma." My mother has never liked it when I broke rules. I distracted her with "I'm dying for you to meet my best friend here, he's a sex- and crack-addicted pedophile. He's a hoot, you'll love him!"

Somehow I made it through family therapy, dinner, and our nightly group therapy session, and I was free. I ran as fast as I could to my dorm and plopped into my tiny bed and chewed through the whole pack of gum before my roommates got home. I was in heaven as I feverishly read "ten ways to stay cool during hot flashes" and a very in-depth article on Beverly D'Angelo. It was fantastic. For the first time in twenty-three days, I was *other*.

guts

When I got home, so much was completely different, yet hauntingly familiar. It's a bit like having déjà vu twenty-four hours a day. *Yes, that's my coffee cup, my couch, my dogs,* you tell yourself. But they feel different, as if they're props in some play. When almost every joyous, sad, upsetting, thrilling, boring, fun, angry, heartbreaking, stressful, celebratory moment since high school has been accompanied by alcohol and drugs, you have to learn how to deal with them all over again. And, at forty, that wasn't easy. I'm still trying to figure them out.

I think that there are many different ways of getting and staying sober. Like religion, I just don't think that one way is the only way. I always think of something said to me years and years ago. I was at a benefit and found myself seated next to an addiction therapist (I know, bummer, right?). I was pretending to be normal, nursing a single glass of shudder-inducing white wine. This was at a time in my life when I was starting to wonder if I might be on the autobahn to nowhere, which is what inspired me to casually clear my throat and say, "Excuse me, sir? I'm just curious. What do you think really keeps people sober?"

He gazed at me over his glasses, which made me think, *Uh-oh, he knows.*

But he just smiled. "That's a good question. And fairly impossible to answer." Then he said something that has resonated with me ever since: "If pushing a peanut up a hill with your nose keeps you sober, well, then, just push a peanut up a hill with your nose."

thirteen

WELCOME TO
THE PLANET OF
THE APES

it's August. The good news is I no longer want to murder people sitting outside at a café daintily sipping white wine. That's pretty much been my lament since May, when I reentered my so-called life in New York. God, I despise drinkers. Don't they realize how annoying they are? *"Ha ha HA*, I can laugh *really* loud because I'm *drunk!"*

Thank God *I* was never like that.

Oh, shut up. Regardless, I really enjoy judging them, it makes me feel superior and less murderous.

Overall, it has been the most treacherous, difficult, exhausting summer of my life. Alone. In the sweltering city. All of my friends either happily nursing their own beloved addictions or snug with their families. My closest friends all on the annual jaunt to a friend's magnificent family compound on a hilltop way above Saint-Tropez, where we guzzled so much of the local rosé, I began simply referring to it as "water." As in "I can't believe I've plowed through six bottles of water and it's not even noon!"

It's the first summer in five years I'm not going, and I know now that I'll never go there again. I'll never get to be with all of my nearest and dearest in one stunning place, laughing through an eight-hour dinner. This fills me with unspeakable sorrow, and *not* just because the rosé was so good.

You see, some of these wonderful, artistic, and insane people are no longer alive, and even though I was already sober, their deaths felt like the final nightcap to one endless, sometimes fun, sometimes nightmarish, twenty-two-year party. The fat lady sang, and it went a little something like "Don't it always seem to go that you don't know what you've got till it's gone."

Loneliness and fear and regret and sorrow have become my new companions. In the beginning, I would wake up every morning and squeeze my eyes shut and pray, *Dear someone. I know I think I don't believe in you, but you'll still help a girl in need, right? Just please help me not to use, and I won't kill myself until tomorrow.*

And slowly, very slowly, the cloak of deep, thick sadness was lifted, *just* enough to navigate that one day. Barely, some days. The relief comes in such tiny doses it's impossible to feel it; until a month has passed and you laugh at a joke. You realize, *Wait, do I feel better?* But you don't dare dwell on it for fear it'll leave as mysteriously as it came.

I diligently, desperately tried to follow everything they told me to do in rehab. I concentrated hard at the meetings I went to every single day, so hopeful that maybe *this would work,* you know? Maybe someday *I* would breezily come to these meetings lighthearted and jovial, cracking jokes and making lunch plans. Maybe someday I'd look as if *I* actually wanted to be there.

I wondered if these people were aware that a lot of the stuff they say makes them seem kinda, well—*drunk.* It's like they've all guzzled the same Kool-Aid, one that removes any savviness and common sense. They talked endlessly about things like *higher power* (Um. Hi? Drunk?) and *rigorous honesty,* which to me sounded like what some rich dumbass would name his sailboat, but instead meant "to tell the truth all the time." Can you stand it? What a bunch of adorable assholes. I'd be laughing if I weren't already crying.

Because, *hello*, everybody lies, *all the time*. Right, don't they? I learned from the time I could talk that life is built out of the millions of lies you tell yourself and especially anyone else. "I'm fine." "Of course I'm happy." "It's not you, it's me." "Really? I thought you *lost* weight!" "Nonsense, who said you're too old for a trucker hat?" Or the handy and well-worn "Your performance left me speechless."

White lies are all I've known since birth. Smile when you're sad, laugh when you're angry, and if an adult says, "The color of snow is orange," then it's damn well orange. I thought every kid was taught this important life skill, along with saying *please* even if you don't mean it and *thank you* even when Aunt Lydia gave you a shitty Christmas sweater for the fifth year in a row.

Therefore, this new world full of church basements crammed with earnest truth-tellers seriously freaked me out. Which is why I was so startled to realize I was actually beginning to be charmed by them. It kind of felt as if I'd discovered a hollowed-out tree in the forest containing singing dwarves.

Then something magical really did happen. I think it might have changed my life in a forever kind of way. Once you've been sober ninety days, you're encouraged to tell your complete tale of addiction to everyone. My idiotic, about-to-be-fired "temporary sponsor" *made* me sign up.

Me? Me. Tell every mortifying thing I've done to a crowd of fellow New Yorkers? I mean, I *just* came clean in rehab three months ago, and that was in group therapy with people I'll never have to see again. Even then I was paralyzed with shame, anxiety, and fear. Even then I minimized it so people wouldn't call their wives and tell them what a loser the tall blonde from *3rd Rock* became.

Seriously, why the fuck can't I just get a cupcake? I mean, why on earth *punish* people for being sober for three months?

I go to a daily 12:30 meeting, which is usually around a hundred people stuffed into a room meant for fifty. A lot of regular crazies like yours truly . . . and, of course, many, many, many utter nutbags. Complete lunatics who say things like "I'm so *grateful* I'm an alcoholic. I just *love* having to be sober every single day for the rest of my life. I wouldn't change a *thing!*"

I'm not from this land of *sharers*, and I am so, so homesick. Where I come from, people don't discuss bad things. I'm desperate to escape back to the New York I've known for the last twenty years, back to the familiar landscape built entirely of booze and bullshit.

Now I understand just how Charlton Heston felt at the end of *Planet of the Apes* when he saw the remnants of the Statue of Liberty and realized that all this time, he was really just trying to escape to where he already *was*. I'm completely overwhelmed with grief and sorrow as I begin to grasp that this is both my ruined past and my new forever.

That morning, I'm more terrified than I can ever remember. So I comforted myself with the knowledge that *of course* I'll exclude the more embarrassing details of my addiction. I'll keep safe all those things so awful and mortifying I've never told another living soul. Right? I mean, who'd ever know anyway?

guts

To my complete bafflement and utter horror, I tell *the Truth*.

All of it.

For the very first time in my whole life. To people I don't know.

I tell *the Truth*.

About lying constantly to everyone who loved me.

About stealing Vicodin all the time from my best friend, who had migraines. About stealing them one Christmas from my mother, who had just had knee-replacement surgery. About taking painkillers prescribed for my own sweet dog. Thank God they weren't beef-flavored, because that would've been *really* embarrassing.

I say everything that I've known for years that if anyone else ever knew . . . well, the shame. The total fucking shame.

The real me was horrified, screaming, *No! Stop it! What the fuck are you doing?* but I was possessed by some completely unknown and terrifying *thing*. A ghastly, truth-telling ghoul who just didn't seem to care about the well-being of the completely fake person that I had worked so hard my whole life to pretend to become.

When it was over, I sat there weeping, in shock and beyond mortified, surrounded by the defeated chunks of my former life. Forty years' worth of lies. I was violently contemplating any immediately available suicide options (can earrings kill?) when all of a sudden I was distracted by something. I looked up to see that people were fucking smiling at me. Nodding. Some of them were crying. And they were all *clapping*. I know they do it for everyone, but it didn't matter. I've had my fair share of applause, but I can say with certainty that never, ever has it meant more to me than it did on that day.

But I haven't even told you the most beautiful moment of all. The memory of it still humbles me and gives me goose bumps to this very day. Up until now, it always felt to me like some people used these meetings to whine or to see how many "sayings" they could cram into three minutes. Therefore I couldn't believe it when, one by one, people raised their hands and started to tell *their* shames, the secrets they had never before said out loud. As I listened to them all, a feeling washed over me that was foreign yet kind of familiar, a feeling from a long, long time ago, a feeling that was almost as good as a fistful of Percocet.

It slowly dawned on me that the feeling was pride. I was actually *proud* of myself for the first time in many, many years. Because by telling the truth, other people did, too.

Me. I did something *good*, for once. I felt something shift, or my molecules reassemble in some new way. That's when I started to understand. If you're somehow brave enough to tell people how ugly you really are inside, people won't hate you. In fact, they respect you. They've all done things that horrified them, that they knew they could never, ever tell.

Just by telling people what an awful person *you've* been you can inspire them to become a better person.

Learning how to tell the truth, for the first time in my life, has been just joyously freeing *and* impossibly awkward. It takes a while to grasp that people don't always want to hear the truth. Jackie summed it up best: "You know, Kristen, just because you're ready to *tell* the truth doesn't mean everyone's all of a sudden gonna be dying to *hear* it." But it makes me feel like I'm becoming a brave, decent person. As if I'm becoming someone I might actually *like*.

I know I have so far to go. I have dreams that I still

don't think I'm good enough to have. I still fuck up constantly.

But that one hour changed my life more than anything else ever has, because it was the moment I finally understood that NEVER EVER AGAIN WILL I ACCEPT THAT SOMEONE ELSE'S REALITY IS MINE, JUST TO MAKE THEM HAPPY.

It also was the moment I was finally brave enough to face my biggest nightmare, revealing the hideous, revolting monster I had tried so desperately to hide from people my whole life. Me. The *real me*.

No one ran screaming from the room. Orderlies didn't whisk me off to Bellevue. I didn't die. The world didn't end.

I simply walked home, the words *I'm enough* pumping over and over through my somehow still-beating heart, and I was who I really am, for the very first time in my life.

epilogue

when I told the people in my life that I was writing a book about my addiction and the events that led to my recovery, almost everyone's reaction was extremely positive. A lucky portion of these people have willingly read this book many times, in many incarnations. An even luckier few were forced to listen to me read every single chapter *out loud*, sometimes more than once. (Don't worry, I kiss your asses in the acknowledgments.) But a few people, who I love and respect dearly, have some very serious misgivings about it. They simply can't fathom why I would expose myself like this when I didn't have to, when most people didn't really know I was an addict in the first place.

Trust me, at first I felt the exact same way. Well, I never imagined I'd even have the balls to *write* a book in the first place, let alone one about a subject I was so ashamed of I couldn't bear to mention it to therapists for most of my life. But something weird starts happening when you get sober. Out of the blue, you find yourself saying yes to things you would never even have considered before. Suddenly, instead of napping, there you are, wholeheartedly agreeing to everything from the ridiculous "Sure, I'll try skydiving!" to the sublime "I'd love to teach acting at NYU!"

Life starts to become fun again. But the best part is, it also becomes scary again. Not the kind of scary you've grown accustomed to, like waking up with two black eyes, a loose front tooth, and ten voice-mail messages letting you know that your totaled car was found last night on the Long Island Expressway. No, this is the good kind of scary, the kind where you can't even believe that you're actually swimming with sharks off the Great Barrier Reef.

It's almost as if you've become an old toddler, unhampered by any preconceived notions of how awful things usually turn out. This innocent stupidity is what led me to agree to write this damn book in the first place. One fine day last summer, I was wandering around my agency, Paradigm, spreading my sparkling wit and dazzling charm to anyone bored enough to pay attention to a forty-two-year-old boisterous baby. That's when Lydia Wills, a literary agent, introduced herself to me and said, "Ever thought about writing a book?"

I laughed and said no, but I told her she was my favorite literary agent ever.

Later that night, I was brushing my teeth and marveling at the fact that I now no longer had pimples. It was much better than that because *NOW* I was blessed with both wrinkles AND pimples. (A few months ago, I even discovered a pimple *within* a wrinkle.) Globs of frothy white dripped from my O-shaped mouth as I dropped my toothbrush in horror. *Oh, no.*

You see, I knew all too well that the combination of pimples *and* wrinkles could mean only one thing: *I was no longer a spring chicken.* And as everybody knows, there is nothing, absolutely nothing, that Hollywood finds more distasteful than a female chicken with no spring. I've always found all the bullshit actresses are forced to do to "stay in the game" (waxy, tight face, fat mouth, extreme dieting) to be completely repulsive. *Well, I'm fucked.*

If you're ever unlucky enough to experience this cruel

and in my opinion totally unfair combination of pimples and wrinkles (or, as I like to call them "pwinkles"), I really hope you're not an actress. Because pwinkles are really just braille for "NO ONE WILL EVER HIRE YOU AGAIN."

My pwinkle terror was compounded because I'd spent most of the last ten years getting wasted, doing plays, getting sober, and teaching acting, and it had recently been brought to my attention that I was very, very close to being "flat broke." Of course, when I received that terrible news, I reacted the way any sane, healthy person would—I promptly went on eBay and bought a huge painting of a monkey smoking a cigar. Because, as an addict, whenever someone tells me I can't or shouldn't do something, a switch in my brain goes off and I immediately think, *Oh-ho-ho, yes I* can.

This becomes quite handy in certain situations. But unfortunately, most of the time I just ended up looking like an asshole with a painting of a monkey smoking a cigar.

And then it hit me. What if I ended up a sober asshole with pwinkles and a bad painting who's *poor*?

I've supported myself since I graduated from NYU, and started making a living acting when I was twenty-five, an age when most of my friends were still living with ten roommates on Avenue C and eating pot for breakfast. I tried to think of what else I could do for a living, and the answer was *not a goddamn thing.* Other than acting, the only jobs I've ever held were "actress jobs" such as waitressing, catering, and a brief stint at the Limited. I'm sure it will surprise no one that I sucked at all of them.

That night I was plagued with frightening, realistic nightmares, always waking up right after uttering, "Hi, I'm Kristen. That's right, I used to be an alien. Would you like to hear the specials this evening?" A black hole of hopelessness and fear began to suck me in.

Then I remembered Lydia, my favorite literary agent ever. *Yes! That's it! I'll write a book! How hard can it be? I love books!* I called her the next morning. We met a week later, and I excitedly told her about the idea I had fever-ishly cooked up the night before, a safe and charming self-help-type book. And I wouldn't have to work too hard or expose myself in any real way. She pretended to be interested and asked to see a sample of my writing. *Oh, shit.* It never crossed my mind that she'd want to read something I *wrote.*

After a long pause—*Think, Kristen, think*—all I could come up with was this nugget: "I'm pretty sure I still have a few of my college term papers. Would you like to read them?"

To her credit, she didn't laugh in my face and instead politely demurred.

Think, chicken, think.

Out of desperation I said, "Well, friends sometimes say I write funny e-mails."

"Forward them to me."

I left the meeting feeling like a total asshole. But I forwarded her a few of the longest ones I could find, and among them happened to be an e-mail I had written my newly sober friend Chris when I had been clean five months.

I knew I'd never hear from her again.

She called an hour later. "This e-mail you wrote to Chris, *this* is your book."

I started laughing. "You have got to be kidding me. Listen, Lydia, I appreciate your passion, but there's no way in hell I'd ever write about my addiction. Ever! *Never ever.*"

About ten minutes later, I started writing and couldn't stop.

guts

I proudly tell people I wrote every word myself, but I'm not sure that's true. It's as if some unknown part of me, some mysterious creature hidden deep inside (the truth-telling ghoul?) was guiding every sentence. I know one thing, though: from that first second I started writing, this book went from just another way to afford more flea market nonsense to mattering far more to me than anything else I've ever done in my entire life.

In some ways, this process was even harder than those months I spent alone in the hospital, because I had to re-live every detail of it while being stone-cold sober. Some parts were so awful that I had pushed them far, far down in my memory. Some parts still make me blush from embarrassment. Besides, I'm an instant-gratification kind of gal, and no one applauds after you've written a good sentence. But as each horrible, embarrassing, funny, or miserable detail was exposed, I found myself feeling lighter, happier, freer. I've never shared the details of what really happened to me in London with anyone until now, and I think it's because a huge part of me still felt that I had gotten exactly what I deserved.

I'd like to make it very clear that I no longer feel that

way. Now, the pride I feel in fighting this damn disease, and in my teaching, acting, writing, healthy relationships, and other accomplishments far outweighs any residual shame I may feel.

By the way, I intentionally chose not to go into a great deal of depth when it came to my loved ones, whether it be friends or my family, because I don't think it's fair to reveal someone else's personal details just because I'm dumb enough to reveal mine. No one has the right to tell someone else's story.

Until they're dead, that is.

There are exceptions to this, stories I felt vital to mine that involved people dear to me. I'm so honored they let me include them, especially the bullying suffered by my brave, kind, and truly gifted brother.

The e-mail I sent to Chris, which started it all, is actually the final chapter of this book, "Welcome to the Planet of the Apes." Admittedly, I've added and removed some parts and fleshed out others. But it's pretty much what I wrote him. It was strange to have the ending done the entire time I was writing. It loomed over my head the whole time. I tried a few other endings, but finally I had to face that it's the only ending this story could have.

Because even though it's the end of the book, that e-mail really signifies the beginning of my life.

It took me a while to realize I didn't just write that e-mail to Chris. I think I wrote it to anyone out there who's struggling to become the person they know they should be. But mostly, I think I wrote it to myself. Almost as if I needed proof, in black and white, that it had actually happened—that I had told the truth and survived.

Recently, I was out in LA for a job. While there, I went to a friend's birthday party and ran into someone I hadn't seen in years. He's a genuinely good man, and I've always adored him, in spite of his career choice (he's an agent). The last time we had hung out, I had been a shit-faced shipwreck. Which is why, after we hugged and told each other how awesome we looked, I was excited to tell him I was sober.

A few hours later, as I was leaving, he pulled me aside and asked me if I wanted some free advice. *Uh-oh,* I thought. *Would it be weird if I said no?*

"Oh-kay, shoot."

"You *really* gotta stop telling everyone that you're sober."

I was completely flabbergasted. "What? Why? I mean, I'm writing a freaking book about it!"

"That's different. I'm just saying that telling people, it could get into the wrong hands, and it could really hurt your career. Besides, it makes people uncomfortable."

I left seething. And feeling as if my hand had been slapped, as if he would have *preferred* it if I had gotten trashed and puked on his shoes. As if I was *supposed* to be embarrassed that I was sober. As if I should keep my mouth shut like a good little sober girl.

It made me feel like a Freak. That's when I remembered that comments like that are the entire reason I wrote *GUTS*. He's probably right, I don't know. But I simply don't care anymore. I refuse to feel ashamed of who I am. I most certainly won't be embarrassed that I'm an addict. So screw my career or my privacy or other people's sensibilities. I'll tell whomever I damn well please.

I don't think we *should* be told to stay silent, locked away in church basements. I think it's time for people to tell whomever the hell they want to about it, whether they're still sick and suffering and need help or are twenty years sober. Or, if you need it to be a private matter, then keep it private. Whatever helps you not to use.

If pushing a peanut up a hill with your nose keeps you sober, well, then, just push a peanut up a hill with your nose.

There's simply no possible way to have a legitimate statistic regarding the exact amount of deaths every year that are caused by drugs and alcohol. I'm not just talking about overdoses, even though those are impossible, too, due to families' embarrassment. But think about all the murders, carjackings, car accidents, suicides, "heart attacks," "accidental deaths," and robberies that occur while the person is high or drunk. If you entered a prison and asked, "Will those of you who *weren't* on drugs or alcohol while committing the crime that got you in here, please raise your hands?"

I promise you, not one hand would go up.

Whether we want to admit it or not, this is *our* black plague, a terrible scourge that's just as deadly as cancer or AIDS. It is destroying people by the untold millions. And

I believe, without a doubt, that the shame and secrecy that shroud the disease are just as deadly as the disease itself.

In my opinion, the best "slogan" when it comes to addiction isn't found in some church basement, or some book. It's a phrase six gay activists from New York City coined in 1987 in the midst of the AIDS crisis: *Silence equals death.*

I won't stay silent any longer.

I hope you won't, either.

The author is donating a portion of her advance from this work to SLAM (Sobriety, Learning and Motivation), a board of New Yorkers dedicated to the creation of New York City's first sober high school. For more information, or to see how you can help, please call (855) SLAMNYC.

thanks . . .

To my mom, who inspired my love of storytelling. (By the way, I'm really sorry for all the F-bombs.) My brother, for giving me permission to share a difficult part of his story. My sister, for laughing at almost everything I've ever said since I was a kid. My dad, for such great memories. And my entire family. Whether we make each other laugh or cry, you're beautiful people one and all, and I'm deeply grateful to each of you.

And then, of course, there's Team *GUTS*:

My aforementioned literary agent, Lydia Wills, for not only convincing me to write this book, but for being able to effortlessly run around Manhattan in six-inch heels.

To everyone at Gallery Books at Simon & Schuster: My editor, Patrick Price, for his keen mind, obsession with formatting, and his heartless (and usually correct, dammit) blue pencil. Kate Dresser, who looks like she should be exchanging witty barbs with Cary Grant in some Capra film and is instead relegated to dealing with people like me. She does it beautifully, and I could never put into words how grateful I am for all of her hard work on *GUTS*.

But there would be no *GUTS* without the soul of my stunning, hilarious, and very wise editor in chief, Jennifer Bergstrom (well, she's wiser than me, sometimes). From our first meeting, her incredible passion for this book was obvious. (I kid you not, she entered the room crying, laughing, and quoting from the two chapters I had sent her. What a dork.) Her support and generosity has never once wavered, and it's meant more to me than I could ever put into words. She's become a dear friend, and I'm excited to prove to her that I'm capable of discussing something *other* than this fucking book.

I'd also like to thank everyone at Paradigm who works so hard for me, especially Sarah Fargo, Erwin Moore, and Jack Tantleff. I owe so much to my friend and manager Becca Kovacik at the Hofflund Company, who has had the misfortune of working with me for almost twenty years. Despite looking like Lily Pulitzer's granddaughter, she's one of the least pretentious people I know. Oh, and Rick Miller, her assistant, for keeping me sane(ish).

To Dr. Barry Cohen, who's not only a terrific and caring physician, but a great human being, who took the time out of his incredibly busy practice to help me make sense of my over seven-hundred-page hospital file. (If there's any medical misinformation, however, the blame lies solely on my shoulders.)

To David Newsom. Whose brilliant photographs (including the cover) added so much to my story. Thank you, truly, for your talent and generosity.

To Dr. Scott Beinenfeld, for his guidance during my sometimes bumpy, always difficult first year of sobriety.

I also have to thank my dear friend Joe Schrank, who met me when I was at my most vulnerable. I don't know what I would have done without him. He's an interventionist, runs the coolest after-care facility in Williamsburg, Brooklyn, and has become an inspiration to me on so many levels. Check out his amazing recovery website, thefix.com.

There are a few friends of mine whose thoughts and ideas really helped me shape this book: Bruce Cohen, Jeff Richmond, Laura Berwick, David Dieguez, Scott Elliott, Wally Shawn, Michelle Lipinsky, Dixie Chassay, and especially Andy Cohen, John Benjamin Hickey, and Joe Mantello.

A special shout-out to Erica Smith, David Khinda, Rob Burnett, and Julie Davis for their annoyingly spot-on notes.

To Marci Klein and Laura Bauer, for being brave enough to help me build my coconut boat.

For their generosity, love, patience, and support, I'm so grateful to Cadee Viele, Chris Miller, Briget Ann Rein, Chris Bauer, Harper Simon, Jamie Tarses, Jason Blum,

Thomas Krauss, John Early, Joe Reilly, Nicholas Famularo, Frank Selvaggi, Kate Moira Ryan, Brad Johns, Tatum O'Neal, Karen Kawahara, Gaetano Romeo, Deanna Swanson, and Kathy Najimy.

To my fairy godmother Wendy Neu. You supported me in such an extraordinary way right when I needed it most.

To her beautiful sister Jackie Bisbee, who's been my best friend since we were freshman at NYU. Thank you for always loving me, especially when I couldn't. Jackie, I've always wanted to ask you something, and for some reason this seemed like the appropriate moment: How the hell have you managed to be such a fascinating, fabulous, and massively successful woman, CEO of your own huge company, have a brilliant husband, fantastic kids . . . and yet remain the least crazy person I've ever met in my life? It's weird. No secret obsessions, no self-harm, no quirks. It's weird, and it's wrong, Jackie. And I'm letting the world know.

To my English friends Daisy and Joanna, who showed me such compassion while I was sick. They were my only regular visitors in the hospital, and would bring me pillows and books. Thank you both, so much.

And to my excellent shrink, Dr. Mary Frederick. I know, it's a bit embarrassing to thank one's shrink. But every time I got scared, or wanted to skate over certain things, or simply wanted to give up on this book altogether, her enthusiasm and excitement were what inspired me to keep fighting to be as honest as I could, and to keep writing. Week after week, I couldn't wait to read the next chapter to her. (Besides, I'll admit, it was nice to have the occasional diversion from having to discuss how fucked-up I still am.) I don't think I've ever met a smarter or more generous person in my life, and it's because of her that I'm continuing the difficult process of trying to live a "mask-free" life.

To Natasha. We all miss you so much. The world isn't nearly as sublime or complicated without you in it.

There are probably so many other people who showed their support in different ways, but due to my prolific drug and alcohol abuse, I can't remember who they are.

So if I neglected to mention you, I suggest you go to an Al-Anon meeting and get over it.

Last, but never least—thank you to all my fellow warriors out there who are fighting bravely to get and stay well. I don't think it makes a difference if you've been sober thirty years, an hour, or the length of time it took you to read this sentence. Remember, we're all just Freaks in the same leaky coconut raft. Hold on. Life just might surprise you if you give it a chance.

Love, Kristen

photo descriptions

Cover photograph, by David Newsom, circa 1997. Taken in his dining room, with no special equipment. As you'll see, there are many photographs taken by David sprinkled throughout the book. This is because not only is he a truly brilliant photographer, but also because we were dating at the time, and he just happened to chronicle me as I began to slide into the darkest depression of my life. Lucky man.

Introduction photograph also taken by David Newsom in 1996. I had just become famous, and I was too dumb to realize that agreeing to be the grand marshal of the Fourth of July parade might be just slightly mortifying. Besides, could no one find a good, old-fashioned convertible? I mean, *a Tracker?*

"I See Nothing, I Hear Nothing" photograph, taken by Chris Miller at a party at Morningwood Farm, Pine Plains, New York, summer of 2006. One of the last photographs I have of me wasted. The expression on my face pretty much says it all.

"The Freak Has Landed" photograph, taken by my father, circa 1978, in our backyard. I was around ten years old.

"Anyone but Me" photograph was my school ID when I was a senior in high school, in 1984–1985. And yes, that's a perm. Deelightful.

"Ye Olde Elvis Catnap" photograph, taken by my dear friend and photographer David Khinda, in July 2011. It was a glorious day, surrounded by friends Kent Cummings, Chris Miller, Karen Kawahara, Gaetano Romeo, Becca Kovacik, and her daughter, Eloise.

"3rd ROCK"-ER SHOCKER" photograph, *3rd Rock from the Sun* photo courtesy of Carsey-Werner, LLC.

"The English Patient" photograph, taken by Erica Smith with my cell phone on June 2010, at the Drama Desk Awards. I had been nominated for best actress for *So Help Me God* at the Lucille Lortel. They hold these prestigious awards in a high school auditorium, hence the PRINCIPAL OFFICES sign.

"Dying Is Easy, Living Is Hard" photograph, taken by Kathy Najimy circa 2000, at her husband Dan's birthday party. What can I say, I was hammered.

"Blink" photograph, taken by my father, probably circa 1967.

"I Think We're Alone Now" photograph, photographer unknown. Late nineties. Taken at a Human Rights Campaign Concert. Let me just say—if you're on stage in a stadium and thousands of gays are loving you, and you still feel lonely . . . ?

"The Suffolk Strangler" photograph, taken circa 1996, by David Newsom.

"The Ghost of Christmas Yet to Come" photograph taken by Natasha Richardson, Christmas 2005. She had convinced me to play Santa that year, and I was so inebriated, I'm surprised Ol' Santy didn't take a tumble. I almost didn't use it because it seemed almost posed to me. But it's real. I think.

"Papillon" photograph, taken by David Newsom in Ireland in 1997.

"Pretty Ugly" photograph, taken by David Newsom in 1997. This one photograph captures the sadness and alienation I felt at the time far better than any words. Not a great year.

"Welcome to the Planet of the Apes" photograph, 2006, taken by Bill Sage backstage at *Aunt Dan and Lemon*, a hit play I did with The New Group.

Epilogue photograph, July 2011 by David Khinda.

Skydiving photograph, taken in 2000. Photographer unknown, but I sure wish whoever the hell it was had managed to take it in focus.

Photo of me and Wilbur, taken by my father circa 1977.

Photo of me pinching my sister Julie, taken circa 1970. I still can't believe my father decided to take the shot as opposed to jumping in to help my poor sister, but I'm guessing he was laughing too hard.

Photo of me and Pinky, 2008, the day I rescued her from the ASPCA.

the end